The Docile Puerto Rican

René Marqués

The Docile
Puerto Rican

Essays Translated with an
Introduction by
BARBARA BOCKUS APONTE

TEMPLE UNIVERSITY PRESS
Philadelphia

860
M357d

Temple University Press, Philadelphia 19122
© 1976 by Temple University. All rights reserved
Published 1976
Printed in the United States of America

International Standard Book Number: 0-87722-048-4
Library of Congress Catalog Card Number: 75-14688

To Puerto Rican youth of today, in the hope that the contents of this volume, which are the product of the pain and the spiritual anguish of a Puerto Rican concerned with the historical destiny of his nation—an American nation—might clarify some fundamental problems which, because of conditions artificially created by others, can be misleading, disorienting, or confusing.

René Marqués
San Juan de Puerto Rico
February 1971

Portico

I need my days to be full of action, and they all pass by without my giving to the world any signs of myself. Each night, on retiring, fearful thoughts accost me, because I ask myself in vain what I have done, what I want to do. Dead, dead, dead. Life without will is not life: to live is to want and to do.

Eugenio María de Hostos

Our genuine surroundings are devouring us because we still do not wish to live profoundly from within our own vital authenticity, from within the most intimate depths of our historic roots. It is a mortal metaphysical aggression against the possibility of one's own being.

Antenor Orrego

I am myself plus my circumstance and if I do not save it, I cannot save myself.

José Ortega y Gasset

Contents

Translator's Introduction

"It is necessary . . . to remind our societies of what awaits them. To warn them that literature is fire, that it means nonconformity and rebellion, that the raison d'être of the writer is protest, contradiction, and criticism."[1] Thus spoke Mario Vargas Llosa, the well-known Peruvian novelist, as he sought to define the significance of Latin American literature today. There is no doubt that an aggressive attitude characterizes the writing of contemporary Spanish American authors, and that a revolutionary spirit underlies much of their work, in both an esthetic and a political sense. Puerto Rican writers conform to this pattern, since most are vigorous critics of the status quo in Puerto Rico and forceful advocates of their country's independence. Like much of Spanish American literature, then, Puerto Rican literature is characterized by a strong social consciousness. Moreover, it is obsessed with a problem not shared, at least to such a degree, by the rest of Latin America—political, economic, and cultural domination by the United States.

This volume of essays, by Puerto Rico's most prominent contemporary writer, René Marqués (b. 1919), represents only one facet of the author's literary efforts. He also is a prize-winning dramatist, short story writer, and novelist. Marqués' greatest contribution has been to the drama, and it is here that the unifying threads of his work are most easily discerned.

Marqués played an important role in the creation of a dynamic national theater in Puerto Rico. He has contributed to its growth not only as a playwright, but as actor, as producer, and as director of the Experimental Theater of the Ateneo Puertorriqueño. Beginning with *El Hombre y sus Sueños* in 1948, Marqués has written thirteen plays. Though their subject matter varies, all of his plays deal with the particular situation of the Puerto Rican people, a situation marked by anguish and alienation, rebellion, guilt, and self-destructive impulses.

The skill with which he gives national themes a profound human dimension and philosophic depth and the variety he achieves by his masterful use of avant-garde theatrical techniques make him one of Latin America's outstanding playwrights.

The focal point of Marqués' plays—and also of his essays—is cultural conflict and the resultant transformation of Puerto Rican society. *La Carreta* (1950), Marqués' most popular play, seeks to depict Puerto Rican cultural reality by dramatizing the successive emigrations of a "jíbaro" family from the country to San Juan, on to New York, and then back to the Puerto Rican countryside. Of course, many Latin American writers argue that modern man can find a new sense of authenticity in the land. So, too, Marqués, in *La Carreta*, suggests that strength is to be derived from the land and decries the false values spawned by modernization and industrialization. In *Los Soles Truncos* (1958), he makes a similar point, this time in a poetic instead of a realistic mode. Two sisters, relics from a bygone era, and unable to resist the pressures of change and of time, are destroyed when they collide with contemporary culture. In *El Apartamiento* (1964), Marqués rejects "modern" values by attacking a society where security provided by the state destroys individuality and creativity. In all three plays, humanistic values are pitted against alien materialistic norms.

The explicit political discussions found in Marqués' essays also have their counterpart in two of his plays. *Palm Sunday* (1949) is a straightforward presentation, in English, of the Palm Sunday killing of Nationalists in Ponce in 1937. In *La Muerte No Entrará en Palacio* (1957), Marqués effectively blends political satire and tragedy. In the play, the governor of Puerto Rico betrays his own people and the ideals of his youth. Thus Marqués is emphasizing the values of national self-sufficiency and self-realization as opposed to the debasing effects of dependency on a foreign power. Other plays such as *Un Niño Azul para Esta Sombra* (1958) and *Carnaval Afuera, Carnaval Adentro* (1962) depict the destruction or sacrifice of innocence and idealism at the hands of the representatives of cynical materialism.

Underlying all of Marqués' dramatic writing is the Puerto Rican struggle to resist the pressures of North American materialism by emphasizing the island's separate identity and special relationship to the Spanish-speaking world. The same is true of his short stories, which have been published in two collections, *Otro Día Nuestro* (1955) and *Una Ciudad Llamada San Juan* (1960), and of his novel, *La Víspera del Hombre* (1959). The latter received the Ateneo Puertorriqueño's

Novel Award in 1958 and the Latin American Novel Prize of the William Faulkner Foundation in 1962.

René Marqués is a contemporary exponent of a long Puerto Rican tradition of nationalist preoccupations expressed in essay form. The essay appeared at the time of the country's first attempts at national emancipation in the mid-1800s. When the century came to a close, Puerto Rico had suffered the trauma of achieving autonomy under one nation, only to become, one year later, the possession of another. Essayists in the early 1900s naturally focused on the possible problems or benefits forthcoming from this new association. But it was not until the 1930s that a generation of writers appeared who addressed themselves specifically to defining the national character. The leading figure of this group, Antonio S. Pedreira, made the most far-reaching attempt at national self-analysis in his book *Insularismo* (1934). The essayist, Juan Angel Silén, thought that "no other book has had such repercussions among Puerto Rican intellectuals and enjoyed more popularity and publicity."[2] Pedreira's *Insularismo* is a direct antecedent of Marqués' essays. As Marqués was to do later, Pedreira sounded the alarm regarding North American influence and singled out docility as a permanent facet of the Puerto Rican character. Pedreira's essay did not spring from a cultural vacuum since other writers such as José de Diego and Manuel Zeno Gandía had preceded him in expressing concern over the essence of Puerto Rico. Nevertheless, it is Pedreira who brought this issue to the forefront of national attention.

Nor was Pedreira the only one to wrestle with the problem of Puerto Rico's identity during the 1930s. One year after the appearance of *Insularismo*, Tomás Blanco published *Prontuario Histórico de Puerto Rico*, which sought, through a synthesis of its history, to explain the formation of the Puerto Rican nation. Blanco's conclusions about the condition of Puerto Rico in 1935 help to show why Marqués has his roots in the thirties generation. Puerto Rico, Blanco said, "lives disorganized by the economic and moral evils inherent in colonialism; controlled by foreign norms, often in conflict with the island reality; disoriented by the lack of concrete and immediately obtainable goals in which it might have faith; incapacitated by the submission of its will to a group of foreign interests . . . . We must either serenely and firmly take our destiny into our own hands, or submit ourselves, like the mentally retarded, to a slow death agony, prolonged by palliatives and orthopedic apparata, until we reach the limits of physical misery and mental prostration."[3] The questions Blanco and Pedreira asked and even the pessimistic prospects that Blanco outlined are those which confront Marqués' generation today, forty years later. This tragic fact will be obvious to whoever studies Marqués' essays.

Many Puerto Rican intellectuals today agree with Marqués that the present moment is crucial for Puerto Rico, and that its colonial status has never been more obvious. They see Puerto Rico as a model of colonialism rather than as a showcase for democracy.[4] What Marqués and those who share his views fear is that the cultural assimilation of Puerto Rico by the United States cannot be stopped, and that Puerto Rican nationality will be destroyed because the process of transculturation has made the indigenous and the foreign indistinguishable. In order to halt this process, today's writers seek to make the defense of national culture a focal point of resistance, since to them at least it is obvious that in Puerto Rico today political and cultural aims cannot be separated. Thus, Nilita Vientós, editor of the magazines *Asomante* and *Sin Nombre*, writes: "The intellectual knows that a nation without political sovereignty lives surrounded by people who tend to destroy the image of its past, a vital condition for it to continue living as a nation."[5] The sociologist Maldonado Denis expresses similar ideas: "Only a people who can make themselves masters of their destiny can confer on present and future generations the roots necessary for a common national identity. The cultural problem we have described is consequently essentially political in its origins and solution. It has to do with the problem of power."[6] Many of Marqués' essays purposely fuse cultural concerns with political ones and his arguments concerning their inseparability are particularly cogent. It seems clear that the Puerto Rican intellectual today feels more intensely than ever before about this issue, and there can be no doubt that the problem of identity and the problem of independence for Puerto Rico will remain inextricably linked in his mind.

Marqués' fervent defense of Puerto Rican culture does not preclude a critical attitude toward some national characteristics. In fact, his most controversial and influential essay is the one in which he argues that docility is a dominant personality trait of the Puerto Rican. He seeks to prove his point by showing how this trait reveals itself in various aspects of Puerto Rican life—psychological, political, cultural, and social. There has been enough material written on the subject for one critic of the theory, Juan Angel Silén, to include in his book a chapter entitled "The Literature of Docility."[7] Nevertheless, Marqués' essay is the definitive one. It is a masterful piece of writing which, despite flashes of humor, presents a devastating critique of the national character. The viewpoint espoused by Marqués is not accepted willingly by the average

Puerto Rican. Thus there was a tremendous public furor when the literary critic Alfred Kazin, a non-Puerto Rican, expressed similar views after teaching for a semester at the University of Puerto Rico in 1960. He wrote: "There is a lamb in the official seal of the Commonwealth of Puerto Rico, and in truth these people are lamb-like . . . . Are they 'docile' because someone has always taken them over—or are they just docile?"[8] Silén, in taking issue with Marqués, calls the latter a colonialist because of his criticism of the Puerto Rican's personality, saying that "the docile Puerto Rican is essentially a colonialist's construct based on a determinist concept," and that Marqués' conclusions reveal a lack of understanding of the capitalist transformation undergone by Puerto Rico.[9] The pessimism found in Marqués' writings and his statements that an analysis of Puerto Rican literature shows it to contain a pessimistic outlook similar to his own have also been challenged, but the majority of Puerto Rican critics seem to agree with him on this.

Another point on which Marqués faces little opposition from his fellow writers is that expressed in his essays in behalf of retaining Spanish as the dominant language in Puerto Rico. The struggle between those who favored English as the principal language of instruction in the school system and those who wished to preserve the primacy of Spanish has persisted since the beginning of the North American occupation of Puerto Rico. Puerto Rican writers have consistently argued that the attempt to promote bilingualism through education is a key weapon of the advocates of Americanization. Silén, for once in complete agreement with Marqués, says that the school system actually creates illiterates in two languages. The points that Marqués makes on this issue are forceful and cogent and have been received favorably by other writers, both Puerto Rican and North American. An interesting comment by Northrop Frye on social mythology, or a society's store of clichés and stock responses, lends credence to the point Marqués is making. Frye writes: "The purpose of social mythology is to create the adjusted, that is the docile and obedient citizen, and it occupies an overwhelming proportion of American elementary education."[10] It is the weight of this educational system and its pressure toward conformity and docility which Marqués combats. Instead, he argues that the young Puerto Rican should have the opportunity to become an informed and active citizen.

In summary, Marqués' essays present a unity achieved by one dominating concern. The defense of Puerto Rico's national identity can and does lead to a discussion of Puerto Rico's literature, of its folklore, of its language and its psychology, and of its relationship to the rest of Spanish America. Central also to this theme is Marqués' view of the mission of the writer: to defend humanistic values, to search for the truth, the truth of his own circumstances, to be a rebel, to be free, and therefore never to abandon the cause of freedom. Puerto Rico can consider itself fortunate in that it has writers like Marqués who alert the nation's conscience, and who unmask the critical problems which must be faced immediately if Puerto Rico is to continue to exist as a nation.

Marqués' essays were first published in book form in 1966. A second, enlarged edition appeared in 1972.

The Docile Puerto Rican

Literary Pessimism and Political Optimism

Their Coexistence in Contemporary Puerto Rico

(An Attempt at Interpretation)

Introduction

One of the paradoxes of Western civilization is that often when a nation's development reaches its peak the intellectual and emotional attitudes of men of letters diverge sharply from those of men in power. They interpret conditions in the world they inhabit from different perspectives, although these conditions obviously are determined by a given set of political, economic, and social factors. Thus, it was precisely when Greece was in its period of greatest military power and political brilliance that the somber Hellenic tragedy flourished. In the Iberian Peninsula, the *Celestina*, the picaresque novel, the *Quijote*, and the bitter irony of Quevedo's writing were products of a period which encompassed the growth of Spain's political and economic empire, from its beginning to its highest point and the start of its breakup. Elizabethan literature, which essentially is devoid of all optimism, reached its extraordinary flowering in the first great period in British history. And today we can observe a very similar situation in the nation which wields the most indisputable economic and political power in the West: the United States of North America. We will attempt to provide an interpretation of the same phenomenon in present-day Puerto Rico. The obstacles and risks associated with this effort are so grave, however, that we must first lay down a few basic guidelines to be shared by both writer and reader.

Exploration of Concepts

First of all, let us explain our basic concepts. When we speak of pessimism, we are not referring to *radical* pessimism as a philosophical

Author's note: The Ateneo Puertorriqueño Essay Prize, 1958. Originally published in *Cuadernos Americanos*, no. 3 (1959); reprint, 1959.

concept of the type identified with a Schopenhauer, a Hartman, or a Leopardi, which became well known during the past century.[1] Instead, we mean a *partial* pessimism that is related to a particular reality.[2] In this sense, pessimism is the expression of a skeptical attitude toward life that does not necessarily exclude any possibility of betterment. In other words, we are not referring to romantic philosophy but to a general intellectual and emotional attitude as old as civilization itself. Its literary expression goes back to Ecclesiastes, a work conceived long before a Hellenized (or Hellenizing) pessimist wrote the biblical Book of Job.

Moreover, when we use the term optimism, we do not mean the philosophical concept expounded by Leibnitz. We use it in its accepted, simplified meaning as an attitude of complacency toward the world in which we live, which is considered the "best of all possible worlds." Translating this into political terms, we would say that optimism is the complacent acceptance of the status quo. Nevertheless, when this tendency toward political conformity is moderate and does not involve fierce resistance to change, it allows for the possibility of improvement, just as is the case with partial pessimism.

Consequently, in the final analysis, the man of letters and the man of action could arrive at a consensus through some type of reformist formula. The difficulty with this is that the censensus usually is to be achieved in the more or less distant future, and to arrive at it the man of letters and the man of action propose to follow different paths. These often are antagonistic, which makes it difficult, if not impossible, to reach a compromise at any given moment.

Terms and Limitation of the Analysis

We do not know of any systematic analysis of the problem set forth in the title of the present essay. Partial studies of literary pessimism abound, especially in North American literature, but they do not deal with its seeming contradiction of existing political conditions.

For our part, we shall limit our analysis to the literary production itself and to its relation, direct and indirect, to contemporary political events. Moreover, as the title indicates, we will deal only with Puerto Rican literature and political developments of the last twenty years. This intentionally narrow focus has an obvious advantage and an equally obvious disadvantage.

The advantage is that the literary material we have examined is readily accessible. With few exceptions, every title is available in bookstores or libraries in Puerto Rico, and can be examined, for purposes of comparison or verification, without difficulty. The disadvantage is that we are dealing with contemporary political events which have not yet been the subject of objective historical research and analysis.

The few attempts at historical interpretation come primarily from official sources or from persons suspected of representing these sources. Their writings are curious examples of a new literary genre, that of "public relations." In the past, this genre was defined with directness and bluntness as "state propaganda."

Since there are no reliable historical texts, the author must depend upon the reader's memory, direct knowledge of recent political events, or firsthand experience with historical occurrences. If these are lacking, the reader will need infinite patience and goodwill as he consults the relevant materials in the few periodical collections of our libraries.

For the purpose of our analysis, we will consider literary pessimism as a social phenomenon, or the reaction of a particular group to specific stimuli from the surrounding world. This focus would seem to contradict accepted psychological theories on the emotional attitude of the writer in relation to the faults or virtues of the world which surrounds him.

It should be clear that our analysis is not concerned with attacking or ignoring psychological interpretations of the phenomenon of pessimistic expression in the *individual*. Instead it concerns the coincidence of many individual pessimisms within a national literature during a specific period. In other words, when a pessimistic attitude occurs consistently in a literature for a lengthy period, it stops being the expression of individual psychologies and becomes a sociological phenomenon.

Antecedents

There is no indication in our literary history that the novels of Manuel Zeno Gandía (1855-1930) were subjected during his lifetime to systematic criticism of their pessimism.[3] This is the case even though the naturalistic esthetic generally attributed to Zeno Gandía caused a definite reaction in literary circles. In other words, the objections to his pessimism may have reflected disapproval of the part it played in his naturalistic style and not of its opposition to a specific political optimism. Nor does it seem that later critics took the trouble to criticize his pessimistic tendency, although they noted that it was a characteristic of his work.

Later in the century, in the valuable and interesting literary production of the thirties, naturalism disappeared. This did not halt the uninterrupted flow of an undercurrent of pessimism in the literature of the period. This phenomenon is evident not only in prose, which we are singling out, but also in poetry, and even in poetry that relies basically on humor and irony. Luis Palés Matos is a good example.

The end of the thirties witnessed the birth of Puerto Rican theater. This theater, which was modern in technique and indigenous in tone and theme, was clearly pessimistic from the onset. Witness *El Clamor de los Surcos* and *Tiempo Muerto* by Manuel Méndez Ballester, *Mi Señoria* by Luis Rechani Agrait, *La Escuela de Buen Amor* by Fernando Sierra Berdecía, *El Desmonte* by Gonzalo del Toro, and even the very feminine comedy *He Vuelto a Buscarla* by Martha Lomar.

At the time, creative writers still were not labelled with the epithet "pessimist." Our environment apparently was such that the pessimism reflected in the literary production of the epoch was tacitly accepted as an appropriate expression of profound national realities.

The Forties: Hope, Accomplishment, Frustration

At the onset of the next decade a current of hope swept through Puerto Rico. The year 1940 brought a dramatic political, social, and economic revolution, which jolted the country and offered a new perspective on present and future possibilities. The adoption of revolutionary socioeconomic measures was the fulfillment of a dream, perhaps not of the people, who rarely dream, but of the country's intellectuals and writers. They were the ones who, together with the men of action, had forged the dream and took the lead in pushing for it to be put into practice. Only one aspect of the dream remained unfulfilled in the first stage: achievement of national sovereignty. Nevertheless, since everyone said that independence was practically around the corner, the creative writers, almost all of whom believed in national sovereignty, let themselves be convinced by the men of action that the struggle for independence could be postponed while the economic and social program was completed.

The plan to be followed seemed politically logical—the nation should seek fulfillment of its ultimate goal once it possessed a solid economic base. The intellectuals fell into the trap. The social and economic development program was carried out, but not with the intent of forging a solid foundation for the final solution. Instead it had the opposite effect. Day-to-day manuevering in the political arena meant that there was rarely time to reflect on basic national problems in a long-range historical context. Consequently, the development program resulted in tying the future of the island, as it never was before in four and a half centuries of its history, to an inescapable and all-encompassing economic dependence on the mainland. Most of the writers associated with the program did not see this in those first years of euphoric enthusiasm. When they did awake, it was already too late.

Optimistic Currents in the Political Thought of the Decade

The initial sense of euphoria was nourished in part by two currents of optimistic thought influencing the new governing classes of the country: on the one hand, Marxist optimism (it was the period when admiration for Russia and Soviet socialism did not constitute a crime against the state) and, on the other, North American capitalist optimism. These two ideologies, which are considered absolutely irreconcilable today, coincide in various ways. Not the least of these is materialist optimism (or, if one prefers, optimistic materialism), which rejects all metaphysics and all implications regarding fatalism or predestination, and thus leaves man free to triumph and be independent in a world created for his entire convenience.

The triumphant man of this optimistic society is always able to dominate his surroundings. The laws of heredity do not even come into play. All men "are born equal," or they are made to believe so. This no longer has anything to do with the political right of equality before the law. Carrying the optimistic fallacy to its extreme, one would come to believe—and some really have believed—that a man of subnormal intelligence can achieve the same goals in life as someone gifted with a superior intelligence. Public education will bring about the miracle. In the North American capitalist society, Dewey and his ideas on pedagogical "progressivism" set forth the guidelines for accomplishing this.[4]

There no longer is room for pessimism or even for skepticism. What man cannot accomplish is accomplished by the machine, which, nevertheless, is carefully labelled the "slave" of man. Life becomes a cheerful marathon to reach the promised land, the materialistic paradise in which everyone shares equally in the supreme happiness. There is no better way to define this state of mind than with the phrase, "the sky's the limit," a product of North American optimism.

Even if this description seems to contain elements of caricature, as indeed it does, it nevertheless is essentially accurate. The central tenet of both optimisms, the Soviet and the North American, is the same and can be expressed as follows: every individual can achieve complete happiness if the state (or society) regulates and dominates the social and economic milieu surrounding him.[5]

Literary Expression in the Forties

What happened in Puerto Rican literature while official life followed the path of optimism? The observer is surprised to note that during the 1940s the literary production of the island continued imperturbably its pessimistic trajectory. This was true not only of the works of writers who had already made a name for themselves, like Enrique Laguerre, Miguel Meléndez Muñoz, Emilio S. Belaval, and Manuel Méndez Ballester (discounting the latter's ineffectual attempt to produce dramatic works of broad popular humor), but of those young writers who were beginning their creative work: Francisco Arriví in the theater, and José Luis González and Abelardo Díaz Alfaro in the short story, to name only a few representative writers of the new generation.

Then, at the end of the decade, the poet and journalist Salvador Tió, an enthusiastic supporter of the party in power, switched unexpectedly to somber humor in his excellent collection of essays, *A Fuego Lento*, published in *El Mundo* and the *Diario de Puerto Rico*. Soon afterwards, the exceptional essayist Tomás Blanco, one of the intellectuals linked to the political movement of 1940 who, consequently, was sympathetic to the government's program, published his quite pessimistic novel *Los Vates* (1949). At the close of the decade, the poet Luis Palés Matos, who till then seemed to support the government, went into seclusion to write poetry which had greater depth and transcendence than his earlier poetry with its emphasis on black themes. His new writings became increasingly pessimistic, relying less on the humor and the irony which he had employed so successfully during the preceding decade.

What had happened? What had caused this gap between literary pessimism and the optimism on which the official world seemed to thrive? Could it be that writers closed their eyes to the reality surrounding them, having decided to shut themselves up in the notorious ivory tower? In our judgment, exactly the opposite occurred. Writers have a sixth sense developed through creative activity and a prophetic vision which, though it may become momentarily confused, never completely disappears. Thus, they had begun to notice realities which were below the surface, signs of danger which the man of action, in his intense daily activity, does not notice, or does not permit himself to notice, because they might disturb the improvised solution he must give to each new problem.

Possible Causes of Pessimism

What events, if any, in the political and social life of the country during the triumphant 1940s might have provoked the discordant note of skepticism, or outright pessimism, adopted by writers concerning the development in progress? We should disregard, as alien to the Puerto Rican scene, two universal catastrophes: the Second World War and the atomic destruction of Hiroshima. Nevertheless, the paradox that it was the sorrow and death of others which brought economic well-being to our country could not escape the notice of sensitive spirits. In fact, without the inflationary economy and the commercial and military needs of the United States during the Second World War, the economic development of Puerto Rico would never have achieved such spectacular results.

But we have decided to limit our arguments to purely local factors. In the mid-1940s the expensive and ambitious state-supported Agricultural Company went bankrupt. This surprising development was a blow to the optimism of an essentially agricultural people. A little later, the agrarian reform program became paralyzed. The effort to recover lands held by large absentee corporations, one of the key points of the "revolutionary" program of 1940, collapsed. In fact the creation of the Industrial Development Company officially stimulated further absentee control of lands. The emphasis on industrialization absorbed so much of the country's attention, energy, and money that, in comparison, the Department of Agriculture could barely fulfill its commitments in those years.

As another means of resolving Puerto Rico's economic problems, the government gave secondary priority to a somewhat unofficial encouragement of emigration by Puerto Ricans to the continent. Finally, in the last years of the decade, an event took place which was to have serious repercussions. This was the violent student strike of 1948, which resulted in the mass expulsion from the University of the leaders of the student movement and of several of the youngest and most brilliant professors. The impartial observer would have to consider the violence employed by the one side to be unusual and the disciplinary measures taken by the other side to be inept. One could already prophesy that the outcome of this university conflict contained the seeds of future problems for society as a whole.

These events obviously did not arise from pure caprice. Undoubtedly, at the time each one occurred, the action taken was justified as politically and economically logical, indeed as a necessary resolution to a dilemma confronting the policymakers. But while they were being advised by technical experts or compelled to take action at a time of crisis, the intellectual, who was not faced with the demand for an immediate solution, could achieve a broad enough perspective to weigh the consequences.

Certain conditions which became apparent to the optimists only during the following decade could already be foreseen during these early years—1) the social ills brought on by precipitate industrialization; 2) a decline in agricultural productivity because of the lack of adequate incentives for production and marketing; 3) the depopulation of the countryside, caused not only by declining employment but also by the stimulus given to migration; 4) the economic ties to the mainland, stronger now than ever, which forced the problem of Puerto Rico's political status toward a dead end; and 5) the destruction in the University of the potential leadership of a whole generation, done not only by terminating the studies of the students who were expelled, but by dissolving the Student Council and creating an atmosphere of fear and distrust in the classroom of every democratic initiative of the student body and even of the faculty.[6]

Something else should be noted, namely a situation which tends to bring forth a reaction of extreme susceptibility in the writer in Puerto Rico or in any country with similar political conditions. This was the growing substitution of foreign values for indigenous ones, which in this case was promoted—if not imposed—by the Department of Public Education and the University of Puerto Rico without any apparent selectivity or appreciation of the adaptability of these values to our culture.

So, there were enough somber events during the 1940s to keep the writer from unconditionally sharing the euphoria of those who embodied the beliefs of the state.

The Decade of the Harvest: Wheat and Chaff

The years after the 1940s could be viewed, politically speaking, as the period of the harvest, the harvest of what had been sown in the previous decade. We say this in general terms, of course, for something else was sown as well. Since in many fields more chaff was harvested than grain, it was necessary to plow up the ground quickly and plant new seed. To be sure, many varieties of this new seed would have been considered useless or, perhaps, dangerous, and discarded automatically from the threshing floors during the 1940s. The sowers will have to wait for future years to judge whether these hasty plantings are to bring about the desired crops.

The next decade opened with two dramatic events. On the local front, there was the revolt of October 30, 1950, which coincided with the Nationalist assault on President Truman in Washington. On the international front, there was the pathetic error of the Korean War, which cost so much blood, so many tears and dollars, but left the two sides in the same position they were in before the struggle. Both events were to have a profound effect on Puerto Rican life.

Let us go on to review, rapidly and superficially, political events of the following years in the island. Pressured by José Figueres, the Governor pardoned Pedro Albizu Campos, who had been convicted of the 1950 revolt. Plans were made for spectacular public festivities to celebrate the adoption of the Commonwealth system.

While the new formula—presumably our salvation—was being acclaimed on the island, in Washington a Puerto Rican who lived in New York carried out a rash act which made the front pages of the world press: Lolita Lebrón fired a pistol at members of Congress while they were in session. In San Juan this led to the re-arrest of Pedro Albizu Campos, accompanied by the usual and always spectacular shootout.

On the economic and social front, industrialization experienced a boom, with the logical consequence of increasing urbanization. New industries, new housing developments, and new suburbs proliferated. For the first time juvenile delinquency became a problem. And efforts were made to copy locally a recent import from the mainland: the "scientifically" organized gang. Drug traffic, which had been minimal, stimulated the circulation of almost as many dollars as industrialization or tourism. And, of course, it is in the industrialized city where dealers, addicts, and intermediaries multiply geometrically.

No doubt, as a kind of compensation, emigration to the continent created something new in North American life, namely the "Puerto Rican problem." New York, to the sorrow of some and the exasperation of others, replaced San Juan as the city with largest Puerto Rican population. A growing number of islanders, who only knew from hearsay about North American racial prejudice, now were experiencing it themselves.

Some sort of judicious equilibrium clearly was being maintained, for the North American colony on the island increased dramatically. Industrialists, professionals, experts, and even skilled workers streamed to Puerto Rico. Their influence was felt everywhere. There was pressure to carry out a more rapid North Americanization of the Puerto Ricans, or, at least, to strengthen even more the already indestructible political and economic links between the island and the mainland. For the first time in twenty years, annexationist sentiments became popular. Once again, North American economic interests exercised a powerful voice, almost equivalent to a vote, over the destiny of the Puerto Rican people.

The harvesting of what had been planted in the 1940s continued apace. At the request of the Governor, the Undersecretary of the Federal Department of Agriculture, Nathan Koenig, undertook a study of Puerto Rico's agricultural system. The study contained recommendations for a sensible and comprehensive program and openly criticized the abandonment of agriculture during the euphoric years of industrialization.[7] Published in 1953, the Koenig report was received with displeasure in official circles. It was not given immediate attention. The press and, consequently, the public were scarcely aware of its existence. But by 1955 the situation in rural areas was so desperate that the Governor finally decided to focus on the agricultural problem by adopting several old plans (and outlining some new ones) to stimulate production and markets. The government attempted to speed up the excessively slow development of the Lajas Valley. This led to the disclosure of basic flaws in the planning and the implementation of the project.

The Government of Puerto Rico paid a substantial sum to a United States research agency to find out what North Americans thought of Puerto Ricans. The result of this expensive study was so dreadful that the Governor ordered it filed away instead of publishing it.[8]

The University of Puerto Rico contracted for the services of a University of Chicago historian, who did not know Spanish, to investigate the nature of North American influence on the local culture. The conclusion of this callow professor, after a three-week personal glimpse of the island, was blunt, namely that there was no such thing as Puerto Rican culture.[9] And this impulsive observer discovered something else in his meteoric visit, namely that Puerto Rico is a country *without history*.

The situation in Puerto Rico during the 1950s could be summarized as follows: an abstruse concept of "associated freedom"[10] had been adopted to calm colonial anguish; grave social problems had followed upon industrialization; agriculture had stagnated (the Koenig report); rural areas were rapidly becoming depopulated; foreign economic interests (absentee or otherwise) were again making their power felt; emigration to the continent was creating a Puerto Rico in exile; migration to urban areas was creating overcrowding with which the Housing Authority could not cope; North American public opinion was disparaging and perhaps openly contemptuous (the Roper report); the island had no culture and no history (Boorstin's conclusions). Under such circumstances, how did Puerto Rican literature express the reality of the decade?

It could be argued that we have concentrated on crass errors, subtle faults, and latent catastrophes to dramatize the point under discussion. That is true. It is likewise true that both the man of action and the so-called "average" man may have been satisfied with the immediate accomplishments of the decade. But writers are not men of action nor "average" men, and in spite of the seeming brilliance of Puerto Rican life, there were enough dark areas during the decade to offend the creative writer's sensibility and keep him from endorsing the fake optimism of official circles.

Aggressive Pessimism in the New Literature, 1950-58

A significant characteristic of the literature of this decade is that in almost all its forms it is no longer merely pessimistic, but aggressively pessimistic. This may be in part because it deals with new themes and problems in a new locale.

With rare exceptions, the writer has shifted his focus from the rural areas to the recently industrialized city. Moreover, the literature addresses itself to three new sources of drama: the Nationalist phenomenon, the suffering of Puerto Rican workers in New York, and the participation of Puerto Ricans in the Korean War.[11] Given these themes, it is to be expected that the literature of these years would not use pastel shades, nor smell of rose apples, nor taste of mango.

This indeed is what happens. By an overwhelming majority, it is the pessimistic works which are best received by responsible criticism and the reading public. It is also these works which year after year are selected in the contests and competitions of the Ateneo Puertorriqueño, in all cases presumably because they have the most intrinsic value or, at least, are most representative of the times. A partial listing, limited to narrative and dramatic works, will illustrate this point.

The first novel of the decade was *Paisa* by José Luis González. It was followed by Enrique Laguerre's *Los Dedos de la Mano* (1951) and *La Ceiba en el Tiesto* (1956). Also in 1956, César Andreu Iglesia's first novel appeared, with the revealing title: *Los Derrotados*.

These were very good years for the short story. Among the volumes published are *Otro Día Nuestro* by René Marqués and *Luces en Sombra* by José Luis Vivas Maldonado, both in 1955. From Mexico, José Luis González contributed a volume, *En Este Lado* (1955). In 1957, Pedro Juan Soto published his collection, entitled *Spiks*. *El Asedio* by Emilio Díaz Valcárcel appeared at the end of 1958.

Newspapers and magazines published the diverse short story production of a group of young writers, prominent among whom was Edwin Figueroa. They also carried the stories of those writers just getting their start in the field, including Arturo Parrilla, Salvador de Jesús, Violeta López Suria, and Ramón Cancel Negrón.

Almost ten years after publishing *Terrazo* (1948), Abelardo Díaz Alfaro published his only short story of the 1950s, "Los Perros," in the magazine *Asomante*. This was as pessimistic as the best of his first collection. In the same issue of *Asomante*, "La Hiel de los Caínes" appeared, by Tomás Blanco, who has dedicated himself sparingly to the short story.

In the theater the decade opened with a somber drama. This was *El Sol y los MacDonald* (1950), which seems to have served as keynote for most later productions, including *El Caso del Muerto en Vida* (1952), *Club de Solteros* (1954), *Bolero y Plena* (1957), and *Vegigantes* (1958) by Francisco Arriví; *La Carreta* (1953), *Palm Sunday* (1956), and *Los Soles Truncos* (1958) by René Marqués; *El Huésped* (1956) by Pedro Juan Soto; *La Muerte* (1957) and *La Hacienda de los Cuatro Vientos* (1958) by Emilio S. Belaval; and *Retablo de Juan Canelo* (1958) by Gerard Marín. The short story writer Emilio Díaz Valcárcel also wrote a drama for television, a piece dealing with the Korean War entitled *Una Sola Puerta Hacia la Muerte*.[12]

The essay during the 1950s did not achieve the pessimistic and prophetic penetration found in Pedreira's *Insularismo* (1934). Instead, it produced the somber humor of Salvador Tió in his collection of essays *A Fuego Lento*, contained in a massive volume published in 1954, as well as Emilio S. Belaval's terse and pessimistic tone in the series entitled "El Intríngulis Puertorriqueño" (1952), which he wrote for the paper *El Mundo*.

It should be noted parenthetically that the 1950s saw the development of a vigorous pictorial movement in Puerto Rico. It was marked by the emergence of diverse tendencies and schools. Nevertheless, so-called figurative art, either frankly realistic or more stylized, seemed to dominate. It is curious that the artists who stand out most within this prevailing tendency share a pessimistic or somber tone, shown in their themes or choice of color. This point is illustrated by the works of painters and engravers such as Tufiño, Rosado del Valle, Torres Martinó, Carlos Rivera, Lorenzo Homar, José Oliver and Félix Bonilla. In the graphic arts only seriography, with its advertising posters, did not follow the prevailing norm. Thus, pessimism is expressed in at least two contemporary artistic mediums: literature and the plastic arts.

Returning to literature, we should note further that two of the writers whose work was well developed in the 1940s tried to give happy endings to some of their more recent works, without very promising results. Enrique Laguerre attempted it in his novel *La Ceiba en el Tiesto* (1956), and it is precisely this forced happy ending which detracts from the verisimilitude and psychological reality of an otherwise fine work. Manuel Méndez Ballester also attempted it in his last drama *Encrucijada* (1958), perhaps with even less good fortune than Laguerre. It is revealing that as originally conceived, this drama did not have the optimistic ending later imposed upon it by the director when it was being staged.

Only one prestigious writer that we know of has attempted to express an all-out optimism in the novel. We refer to the well-known poet and essayist José A. Balseiro, who lived in the United States for many years. He published a very mediocre novel, *En Vela Mientras el Mundo Duerme,*[13] which is the only apology for the status quo in contemporary Puerto Rican literature.

The works mentioned above constitute only a fraction, although a substantial one, of the literary production in prose during the decade. Nevertheless, quite clearly the bulk of it is characterized by pessimism.

A Generational Phenomenon or a Literary Style?

It should be noted without evasion or preamble that we are not dealing in any way with a generational phenomenon. During the periods under discussion, three generations have been active. To a greater or lesser degree, their spokesmen, adopting distinct points of view, interpret Puerto Rican reality from a pessimistic perspective. Sometimes the writer tries to escape his immediate circumstances, placing his work in more or less exotic places, as for example in Belaval's *La Muerte*. But even in such cases, he cannot avoid a pessimistic outlook caused in large part by a vital experience connected with the same reality from which he has attempted to flee.

We also are not dealing with a literary style imposed by postwar pessimism and imported from literary groups rendering homage to a Jean Paul Sartre or a William Faulkner. French and North American literature may have influenced technique and style, especially in the younger generation. But a pessimistic perspective cannot be imported into a literature, just as one cannot import literary optimism. No matter what the technique and style of the writer, the themes he chooses emphasize shadowy zones of reality. This is an indisputable fact. Writers as different in style and technique, in ideology and in cultural background, as Laguerre, Soto, Belaval, Arriví, Salvador Tió, Andreu Iglesias, Díaz Valcárcel, José Luis González, Tomás Blanco, Abelardo

man in power through the abrupt dismissal of the Chancellor by the Council on Higher Education. It is only fair to note that the Governor actually attempted this solution; only it was not easy any more.

Chancellor Jaime Benítez of the 1950s was not the Jaime Benítez of the university strike of 1948. Then he had needed all the weight of the government machinery, mobilized by the head of the majority party himself, in order to quash the movement. But over the years, the incumbent of the chancellery had grown enormously in prestige and political power. He was supported by the now strong annexationist sector on the island, including the influential newspaper *El Mundo*. In the United States, he had the support of multimillion dollar foundations and prestigious teaching institutions. Moreover, his expensive publishing enterprises and his ability to handle so-called public relations had extended the prestige of the Chancellery to Spain and Latin America.

For his part, the Governor, who originally was an egalitarian democrat, had become more of a liberal democrat. When he failed in his first attempt to force a resignation, he was prevented from taking drastic action by the obvious power of his foe and his own new liberal attitudes.

Thus began the struggle between the Chancellery and Fortaleza, the Governor's residence. It has lasted for years and its farcical aspects could not escape the most naive observer. This celebrated, albeit artificial, polemic of "Puerto Rican-ism vs. Westernism" was used satirically in three literary works: *Juan Bobo y la Dama de Occidente: Puerto Rican Pantomime for a Western Ballet* (1956), *La Ceiba en el Tiesto* (1956), and *Retablo de Juan Canelo* (1958).[14] The authors belong to different generations, which would explain their different approaches to the theme.

Nevertheless, the official farce had two healthy indirect effects. It forced the University, for tactical reasons, to give more importance to Puerto Rican values, and it helped to focus the attention of the always sleepy public on the problem of instruction.

The spotlight finally fell on something the honest intellectual had clearly perceived. Public education—particularly at the primary and secondary levels—is one of the fields where we get the poorest returns in relation to the effort, time, and money invested. Although at first glance the picture revealed by statistics is spectacular, a more careful examination shows that in the last twenty years the net achievements of the educational system in terms of quality and social utility are little less than a fiasco.

Because of intricate political factors too tedious to mention, but arising from the situation described above, the Governor was forced to announce a revision of the school system. We still do not know what seeds, new or old, will be planted in this newly opened furrow.

An official policy of encouragement and promotion of the arts was unexpectedly promulgated at the same time. The plastic arts in particular received generous aid from the government. The Ateneo Puertorriqueño for the first time in its history was favored with an official subsidy. At the initiative of the Governor, the Institute of Puerto Rican Culture was created. The literary magazine *Asomante* also received an appropriate subsidy. The First Theater Festival, like the Casals Festival, was organized. Finally, a symphonic orchestra was founded under official auspices.

In the political realm, the Governor's new liberalism led to two dramatic actions. He named a commission presided over by the jurist Mr. Baldwin to investigate civil rights in Puerto Rico, and he decreed a campaign of democratic housecleaning to combat the "bossism" rampant within his own party.[15]

Moreover, he proclaimed a new doctrine—Operation Serenity. If the 1940s were years of action (Operation Bootstrap), the years which remained of the 1950s were to be dedicated to something defined as "serenity" (meditation? contemplation?). A little later, it was solemnly affirmed that the world now lived in an era of postnationalism (in spite of the fact that Asia, Africa, Latin America, the Antilles, and Europe were ablaze with nationalism). Puerto Rico was declared an international meeting ground.[16] Because of this, and with the enthusiastic help of the Department of State in Washington, San Juan periodically plays host to official visitors. They come not only to take part in conclaves, forums, and conferences, but also to admire and, naturally, to applaud the spectacle mounted in the Caribbean, which the Governor himself has baptized with the revealing name of showcase of democracy.

Official interest in the arts has resulted in a veiled attempt at state control. The so-called "unjustified" pessimism of contemporary Puerto Rican literature is beginning to elicit reproach. The pessimistic attitude of the writers, it is said, does not reflect the dynamic reality of the Commonwealth nor the complacent conformism of a "grateful and happy" people.[17]

Interpretation and Prophecy

The shrewd observer can easily perceive that the overall picture is one of pitiful chaos. Every government has the right, in fact an absolute duty, continually to revitalize itself. It seems to us, however, that in the case we are studying, the measures taken along these lines are overdue on the one hand and premature on the other.

They are overdue in the sense that the errors which they try to correct have grown deep roots over a long period of twenty years. To correct these errors would require at least as long a period of time in the future.[18] It goes without saying that there is no possibility of the Governor's being succeeded by a series of political heirs. The party in power *is* Luis Muñoz Marín. On his death the precarious cohesion among his followers, whom only he has been able to keep free from dissension and a total breakup, will disappear. The subordinate figures will exploit his name as they divide up pieces of the edifice. The total edifice, however, with its accomplishments and its faults, will die with the man. The pity of it all is that the Governor could not rectify these flaws during his remaining time in power, even if he were conscious of them and honestly wanted to correct them.

From a different perspective, this so-called process of rectification can only be interpreted as being premature. The recent new directions, proclamations, declarations, and attitudes are appropriate for a government of a people who have arrived at a definite goal, for a people who finally have found their political destiny. Are these attitudes and declarations attributable to a political posture that seeks to make precisely this impression? Or do they originate with an exhausted government which, after twenty years of accomplishments and failures, desperately longs for rest, and peace?

Whatever the answers to the previous questions, the main fact is clear: Puerto Rico has not arrived at its goal. Its unresolved political destiny is as much of a corrosive cancer in today's social structure as it was in previous decades.

The fact is that political events of recent years provide sufficient basic information to enable us to offer a prophecy: the Governor can expect anything but serenity in his remaining years in power. Apart from his failure to convince the thinking sectors of his country that the Commonwealth constitutes a viable political formula, there are old economic problems still unresolved and new social problems developing with frightening speed. The door which he thought to open with the old reformist formula of "associated freedom" has brought him up against an insurmountable wall.

His fifteen years of preaching against national sovereignty has not resulted in acceptance of the status quo, as was his obvious intention.[19] Instead it has stimulated as a logical consequence the devastating growth of annexationist ideology. With the now inevitable disappearance of the Independence Party, the ineffectual but at least "democratic" channel for the ideal of independence, two dangers face the Governor. On the one hand, there is a resurgence of Nationalist intransigence and on the other there is a menacing growth of the Statehood Party, the advocate of annexation.

The encouragement of cultural nationalism will not lessen the yearning for national sovereignty of those who favor independence, and much less that of the Nationalist fanaticsm. Besides, having misused the term "free" in his reformist formula, the Governor can only struggle now with the qualifier "associated." And the struggle is shaping up as so intense that there will be no possibility for quiet enjoyment of an Operation Serenity.

Present-day annexationism—the most immediate political danger for the Governor—is his own creation. A latent fifth column within his own party, annexationism is supported unconditionally by the most prestigious newspaper in the country and by the power of the large companies, both local and North American. Not surprisingly, the increase in the electoral strength of the Statehood Party (annexationist) in the last elections was little less than spectacular.

Ironically, it will not be independence—which was feared and combatted so much—that in the end will destroy Muñoz and his work, but annexation—the opposite political pole.[20] It is no longer rash to predict that, sooner or later, the annexationists will succeed Luis Muñoz Marín in power. Of course, once in office, they will not hurry to implement the policy of annexation. It never would be conceded to them anyway by the North American Congress. The ideal of independence once again will become a force to be reckoned with in the electorate. And the eternal colonial cycle again will repeat itself, as it has been repeating itself since Puerto Rico became conscious of its own being. That covers the political aspect of the prophecy.

Now, will the notorious absence of consonance between the creative artist and the man of action continue in the next decade? Will the Puerto Rican painters continue highlighting in their paintings and engravings the miseries of the San Juan slums, while the tourists toast themselves in luxury resorts beneath the tropical sun? Will Puerto Rican writers continue to cry out gloomily against the complex social and psychological problems inherent in industrialization, while official statistics proclaim the economic benefits of industrial development? Will dramatists and narrative writers continue exploring the Nationalist phenomenon while the Governor proclaims that the world has entered a happy postnationalist era? Will Puerto Rican literature continue to grieve over the uncertainty of the country's political destiny, while the government affirms that it has definitively resolved this corrosive condition? Finally, will the perception of reality of the poet and the man of action continue to be distinct? Will political optimism and Puerto Rican literary pessimism continue to be irreconcilable? We think so. In the first place, the poet's time undeniably is prophetically several beats ahead of the politician's. In addition, there are special circumstances in the present Puerto Rican situation which, taken together, justify the lack of optimism of the active writers.[21]

The Reaction of the "Average Man" to Literary Pessimism

Up to now we have tried to examine the paradox by relating it directly to those who are responsible for it: the man of action and the creative intellectual. It is worth noting the reaction of that other person who, in the last instance, is the raw material with which the politician always works, and sometimes the writer. We refer to what statistics today monstrously call the "average" man, but who in the past we simply called John Doe, showing in that way greater humanity. What does he think, if he thinks at all, about the pessimism in our literature? Or, at least, what is his emotional, not intellectual, reaction to the problem we have posed?

Obviously this is difficult to determine. Narrative and dramatic literature is not a vital experience of the "average" citizen in our society. Literature and theater in Puerto Rico attract a scant following. This point can be emphasized without considering its causes since, whatever they are, they do not affect the terms of our exposition.

As we pointed out before, the intellectual minority capable of esthetic judgment seems to prefer pessimistic literature. But this group's capacity for esthetic judgment may invalidate the analysis. In fact, the reader and the cultured spectator would prefer works with the highest esthetic value independent of their pessimistic or optimistic content. That is to say, even if the qualified reader or spectator is inclined intellectually or emotionally toward optimism, his integrity prevents him from preferring an optimistic work with esthetic values inferior to those of a pessimistic work. Therefore, unless a scientific analysis is undertaken regarding this point, the final answer to the problem will always remain mere speculation.

Fortunately, we do have such an analysis. Moreover, the analysis refers not to the so-called cultured minority but, precisely, to the "average" man. We are talking about the results of research carried out in the rural sector by the Analysis Unit of the Division of Community

Education with respect to the pamphlet *Los Casos de Ignacio y Santiago*.[22] The study was prepared by the specialist Angelina Roca, based on principles followed by the University of Michigan at Ann Arbor and adapted to local conditions.

The pamphlet *Los Casos de Ignacio y Santiago* contains two short stories with identical educational messages. The focus of the first story, "La Voluntad que Ignacio no Tuvo," is negative (pessimistic) and that of the second, "Santiago Vence al Ratón," positive (optimistic).

The educators wished to emphasize the following issues in each message: contaminated water, leadership, and the timidity of the farmer about participating in the solution of communal problems. Treatment of the second issue was somewhat muted because it dealt with a touchy question. In the two stories there is a close parallel in the psychology of the protagonists and in the dramatic situation which both confront. But the history of Ignacio has a "tragic" ending (the death of his son from contaminated water, a communal problem which Ignacio, because of his timidity, does not decide to solve). Santiago's story has a happy ending: his little son is saved because he, conquering his timidity, helps to solve the problem of the contaminated communal water.

The conclusions of this study are revealing.[23] There are several extremes, which do not interest us here. Apart from these, the results of the analysis, as they relate to the comprehension of the message and to its dramatic and emotional impact, tend to favor the pessimistic story. Thus, the educators discovered that the preconceived idea that an educational message can only be effective if it is presented positively (an optimistic focus) was a fallacy. What interests us, of course, is the discovery that the "average" man (at least the one in our rural areas) seems to identify, intellectually and emotionally, more closely with the pessimistic rather than with the optimistic focus.

Therefore, we can reasonably conclude that the pessimism of our contemporary literature is not as remote from the people as some try to make us believe. Furthermore, one can now say with certainty that the literary pessimism, while it may not "syncronize" with official optimism, is the "syncronized" expression of profound psychological realities of the Puerto Rican people.

Is Literary Pessimism a Destructive Force in a Society?

In the preceding discussion pessimism and optimism often appear as antagonistic, almost irreconcilable forces. Put that way, such an exposition could be interpreted as a tacit agreement that literary pessimism is a force as negative and destructive for society as political optimism is positive and healthy. Of course, this is not the case. We have already seen that to obtain a positive and healthy result (the complete understanding of a specific educational message), educators can effectively use a pessimistic literary focus.

Why then does the state, any state, if it becomes aware of literature as a social factor of some importance, demand or at least ask that literary expression be optimistic? Is it perhaps because pessimism in literature can be capable of destroying a people, or harming a society? From Ecclesiastes to the Book of Job, continuing on to Greek tragedy, to the *Celestina* and the *Quijote,* to the most imperishable of Elizabethan plays, and to the notorious pessimism of contemporary North American novels and theater,[24] a case has never been recorded where literature of a pessimistic type in itself threatens national stability or adversely affects the well-being of a people. Literature has never had such power. It receives but does not create historical, political, or social conditions.

Literary Optimism: A Necessity of the State

It is this receptive quality of literature that accounts for the preoccupation of the state or, more precisely, for that of the party in power. Since literature is the poetic transmutation of existing realities, literary pessimism has to be uncomfortable, if not downright irritating, for the state. It is not politically desirable to those holding power for the negative or somber aspects of the status quo to be exposed to the public eye, even beneath the winged mantle of poetry.

From this point of view it is understandable, though not excusable, that the head of state might reject all literary pessimism and, if the state had such a power, that he would declare it subversive, and punish it. Without entering into the moral or ethical aspects of such an action, we have to recognize that from a strictly political point of view, in which morals and ethics usually are not determining factors, the ruler acts in self defense. This is so because while literature does not harm *societies,* nor destroy nations, in the long run and in specific circumstances it can undermine the foundations of a *government.* It can do this by giving the people, or at least an appreciable sector of the ruling class, a clearer perception of negative conditions previously unnoticed or unknown.[25]

On the other hand, pessimistic literature could strengthen the same government to which, directly or indirectly, it is a living reproach. It could serve this purpose, if, instead of assuming a defensive attitude, the state would pay attention to the reproach by analyzing its causes, studying the social or political faults implied in it, and, finally, finding an adequate solution for them.

The Ethical and Moral Mission of the Writer

This possibility raises another problem. We frequently hear categorical statements to the effect that a writer is pessimistic because of purely personal frustrations, or that he romantically chooses pessimism for the pessimism itself, or even that he "amuses" himself with his pessimism and that his enthusiasm is worthy of a better cause. Of course, temperamental or psychological factors can predispose an individual toward a specific intellectual or emotional reaction to the surrounding world. But discounting these, we must conclude that these statements express an ignorance of two fundamental facts: the authentic mission of the creator in the society which gives him his "raison d' être," and the complexities of the creative process.

The difficult mission of the creative artist is not to illuminate that which already is bathed in light. This is especially true in societies like Puerto Rico, where it is difficult to delimit clearly the zones of light, shadow, and semidarkness. That is to say, in complex societies like ours it is useless to make the simplistic distinction between the morally black and the morally white that is so easy in obviously dictatorial regimes. Because of this, in Puerto Rico the writer has to keep his powers of perception extremely sharp in order to capture the subtle differences which escape the notice, not only of the masses, but even of considerable sectors of the ruling classes.

Now, when the writer emphasizes those shadowy zones which he discovers in the surrounding world or in himself as a reaction to that reality, he does not do it to amuse himself, but to bring to light, to expose and denounce what is hidden. He thus fulfills his moral and ethical mission.[26]

But what lies behind this mission? Or, framing the question another way, what drives the creator to expose or denounce an evil? There is only one answer: the hope that the evil denounced will be eradicated; the hidden hope that the exposition of the evil will provoke the search for a solution. The somber and anguished questions which the pessimistic writer formulates do not have the evil purpose of plunging man into desperation and nothingness. On the contrary, he formulates them as a challenge to man's creative capacity; they are darts shot at the sleeping conscience of others. This is true both of the questions which deal with social, economic, and political matters and of those which approach the metaphysical, it being understood that in the latter case the one interrogated is God.

What I bring to Your attention—the writer seems to say, whether it be to God or to man—is a defective part in something You created.

What do You plan to do about it? Do You not think, as I do, that the problem deserves a solution? Is it not time now for you to begin to perfect Your work? What are You doing there, contemplating in fascination Your divine navel, so complacent and pleased with yourself, when there are things such as these threatening the health of Your kingdom?

In fact, what in the last analysis is tragic literature, from its Greek beginnings until the present, but a series of denunciations of evils unleashed by men and gods? Fatality, Destiny, Man, Society, State, God, the name does not matter, the pessimistic writer always presents his implicit or explicit denunciation to this someone whom he believes responsible and from whom he hopes to obtain—a hidden faith, a secret hope—an answer, perhaps a happy solution.

The Pessimistic Writer: An Optimist

We are now in a position to state directly a surprising theory: the pessimistic writer can be, and usually is, an optimist. It is precisely his optimism, and even more his meliorism—his faith, confessed or not, in the possibility of change, of a solution—which inclines him toward a literary pessimism. Even in the extreme case of a misanthropic or atheistic writer, he seems paradoxically to conserve an unconfessed faith in the possibility of moving to action those beings whom he denies: man or God. Think of Solomon, Cervantes, Quevedo, Shakespeare, Freud (in what this Viennese had of the poet), Neitzsche, Dostoevski, Faulkner, Sartre, Camus. Certainly the son of David, sick of life and of men, would not have taken the trouble to write the Ecclesiastes if he had not held the secret desire to point out to man—from his personal and bitter store of wisdom—a harder but surer path to perfection.

The Sound and the Fury of
Mr. Kazin's Critics

Have pity, Lord, have pity on my poor people!
On the dead waters of these simple souls' lives
Let a ruffian throw the redeeming stone of a disturbing deed.

Luis Palés Matos

An alert Puerto Rican observer could not fail to find highly amusing all
the sound and the fury provoked by Mr. Kazin's observations on today's Puerto Rico and Puerto Ricans.

The fact that much of the fury comes from well-intentioned members
of the American colony in San Juan somehow adds to the humor of the
situation.

Objecting to the visiting critic's article, most of these friends are careful not to argue about the unflattering comments he makes about North
Americans in Puerto Rico, or about his even more unflattering interpretations of the United States' role in the contemporary world. Like
new Quixotes they prefer to defend the poor Puerto Ricans from Mr.
Kazin's attacks. We, the attacked, should no doubt be deeply moved
and most grateful for this very Christian attitude of the North American
colony in our country.

I must confess that I fail to be either moved or grateful for the

Translator's note: Where possible, I have used Mr. Marqués' original English version
of this article, which had been revised and translated into Spanish by the author for its inclusion in the collection of essays.

Author's note: This essay first appeared, in its English version, in the *San Juan Star*
(March 8, 1960) as an answer to the article "A Critical Look at Puerto Rico," by the
North American literary critic Alfred Kazin (a visiting professor at the University of
Puerto Rico for a brief period), and to the bitter criticism that his commentaries provoked
in San Juan. "A Critical Look at Puerto Rico" was published in New York's *Com-
mentary* magazine, and the *San Juan Star* then reproduced it, two weeks before René
Marqués' answer in the same newspaper.

generosity of these fellow citizens from the continent, perhaps because I have not yet read any comment on Mr. Kazin's article which gets to the core of the matter.

A tacit agreement seems to prevail among these critics to distract attention from the fundamental problems exposed by the American writer. They emphasize, significantly, superficial and secondary details, such as his silly remarks about the ice creams or sherberts which are sold from "musically" annoying trucks, about metropolitan noises, and about the monotonous uniformity of the stucco houses in the recent United States-style housing developments. (Here Kazin is right as to the imitation and monotony of the local suburban architecture, but in error as to the stucco, since concrete is the material of construction and ornamentation which is used and has been used for years in the "new" Puerto Rico.) There are, however, more important things than these banalities in Mr. Kazin's article, and I suspect that his critics know it very well, though they may pretend to ignore it.

Weak Points and Blunders

Obviously, there are quite a few weak points and some blunders in Mr. Kazin's statements. He is not, after all, either a sociologist or an historian. He does not even pretend to give a "scientific analysis" (whatever that is) of Puerto Rican society, but merely an impressionistic one. He does, however, base some of his information on Professor Richard Morse's supposedly scientific analysis, which was in turn a reply to the "scientific analysis" of some other North American expert, who was supporting or contradicting the "scientific research" of another more remote imported expert, in that sterile chain of supposedly scientific bickering which is repeated ad nauseam in the University of Puerto Rico. The native Puerto Rican is a favorite guinea pig for North American specialists in the social sciences. He seems to them a spectacularly astonishing being because he has been able to live in society, assimilate civilization, and re-create culture, art, and folklore long before General Miles arrived on our shores in 1898.

Furthermore, although he is a good writer, Mr. Kazin could not be called a polite one. (What possible good a polite writer could do in this savage atomic age is a very pertinent question in relation to what occupies us here.) As a person, moreover, Mr. Kazin lacks human warmth. No Puerto Rican who attended his lecture in the University of Puerto Rico would label him as "simpatico." Therefore, in spite of his academic preparation and his writing ability, he is not a good university professor and most certainly is a disorganized and, what is worse, very dull lecturer.

Granting all that, should we hastily dismiss in toto Alfred Kazin's observations on Puerto Rico and the Puerto Ricans? Why should we? Why not admit that some of the opinions expressed by an "antipatico" North American may be more valid and more genuinely truthful regarding our present situation as a people than the flattering or charitably patronizing chatter of so many North Americans who insist on being "understanding" and "charming" to us? Is it that our ingenuousness obliges us to appreciate less the brutal honesty of the former than the sly hypocrisy of the latter? Are we, Puerto Ricans as well as Americans living in Puerto Rico, so touchy and immature that we cannot swallow anything but sweet words or sugary praise?

It seems that what some Americans have resented most is Mr. Kazin's statement about Puerto Ricans being docile. But aren't we? Needless to say, as a Puerto Rican, I hate to admit it. But being honest, I have no alternative but to accept it.

For the last twenty years we have all heard Governor Muñoz Marín praise most enthusiastically our docility (only he calls it our "peacefulness"). I have yet to hear a North American in Puerto Rico, or even a Puerto Rican, dispute that conclusion of Mr. Muñoz Marín. Furthermore, whenever the Nationalists have tried to step away from what is considered the Puerto Rican stereotype of docility, we have heard the unanimous cries of apology coming from Americans and Puerto Ricans alike: "That is not typically Puerto Rican! That is an exception! The Puerto Ricans are a very, very peaceful people." So?

So we are docile. Had we not been, Puerto Rico would have attained its national sovereignty in the nineteenth century. Had we not been, the Puerto Rican masses would have become Nationalists and would have supported Pedro Albizu Campos in the thirties, when his Nationalism seemed to be the only decorous and dignified way out of our colonial confinement. Why didn't they? Perhaps because those masses were "objective," "scientific," "pragmatic," and so forth in their evaluation of the political situation? No. Simply because they were what Governor Muñoz Marín calls "peaceful" and Mr. Kazin "docile."

I will leave for a better occasion a discussion as to whether docility is to be interpreted as a negative or positive characteristic of a people.[1] The fact remains that we Puerto Ricans can be antisocial, defiant, or merely nonconformist on occasion and even heroic in some cases *as individuals,* but we are certainly docile as a people. I do not see why Puerto

Ricans (and least of all North American residents) would take such pains to deny the fact. (A guilt complex, perhaps?)

An Explanation of Puerto Rican Docility

Mr. Kazin's perception and insight seem to run away from him, however, when after pointing out the phenomenon of docility, he leaves it up in the air, without any attempt at interpretation. But perhaps we should not ask that much of the North American writer's article. His piece is descriptive, not interpretive.

We Puerto Ricans, of course, could substantiate with historical data the phenomenon he points out. Docility is, of course, primarily an acquired rather than an inborn trait. Puerto Ricans are today docile simply because they have been, since the beginnings of their history, a colonial people—a people entering the life of the Western world from the humblest social strata of sixteenth-century Spain. In contrast to the colonial experience of other regions, Puerto Rico was colonized by a handful of modestly laborious or frankly indolent people who had learned docility in Spain, given their inferior social condition within the rigidly stratified European society of the period. With them were to be mixed, without too much effort, two primitive ethnic groups, made docile by forced labor and slavery: Tainos and Africans. This country, so constituted in its origins, and of little demographic density during its early centuries, would develop a sense of helplessness which sprang not only from its inferior political status, but also from its physical isolation as a small, remote, and apparently poor island in comparison to the fabulous riches—discovered, plundered, and noisily proclaimed—of Mexico, Peru, and other regions of America.

Under both regimes, Spanish as well as American, this ancestral sense of helplessness and impotence was and continues to be psychologically exploited to the maximum through education, as always happens in any colonial society. Modern methods have not changed the basic aim, although the process of "docilization" may be more subtle. From kindergarden on, public as well as private education deprives the Puerto Rican child of his national pride, of that necessary and vital feeling that *he belongs to something immediate and definite in time and in space,* of his history and tradition, and of the self-respect of being part of a country and a people that are *his* (truly his, not of *others*): Puerto Rico. Any positive accomplishment or action carried out individually by a Puerto Rican or collectively, when it is not belittled or denied, is always attributed, directly or indirectly, bluntly or subtly, to the fact that we belong to (more recently and hypocritically the expression is "we are associated with") an all-mighty, all-powerful, and infallible nation, as generous as God himself (once Spain, now the United States).

The schoolchild soon learns to develop a very adequate and proper inferiority complex. According to what he is taught, Puerto Rico is doomed for eternity to be a *part* of something bigger than the island itself. Puerto Rico is not and never will be something by itself: only a dot, a fly speck on the map of the world. "Do you see all the progress Puerto Rico has made?" teachers ask in English and Spanish. "Well, not even a minimal fraction of that great progress would be possible for us if Puerto Rico had not had all the advantages of the generous protection and the loving care which the United States showers upon us. Do you realize how democratic and how peace-loving our local government is? That is because we are part of the United States. Were we politically on *our own*, we would have a murderous dictator in Fortaleza and ugly and bad Puerto Ricans would be killing nice and charming Puerto Ricans and even nicer and more charming North Americans in the streets. Yes, yes, as ugly people do all the time in Asia, Africa, Latin America, and Europe. These horrible things would happen here *too* if Puerto Rico were to be *left alone*. We would not know how to live together. We would kill each other. And we would starve, too! Yes, my child, only the glorious (may it be blessed!) American flag in Puerto Rico prevents all these awful, frightful things from happening in this dear, but so small, poor, and defenseless little land of ours." The teacher, having as a background the picture of Washington, Muñoz Marín, or Johnson, and after stating what the system has taught him or her to say, feels choked up by emotion, and falls silent. His (or her) unhappy students shudder with terror before the devastating apocalyptic vision so eloquently presented by their noble mentor and now know that they can never nor will ever desire to be Puerto Ricans; that their destiny as children of the colony of Puerto Rico will fatally lead them to be authentic, loyal, unconditional North Americans, because only in this way—they understand this well now—will they be able in the future to save their tender skins and their delicate stomachs.

The above is obviously a caricature. But, like every caricature, it only exaggerates in its general lines what is fundamentally true about colonial education in Puerto Rico. Raised and educated to be docile, why should the Puerto Rican be otherwise? And why on earth should it be the North American residents here who appear to resent most bitterly Mr. Kazin's statements as to what we are?

A Denial of Puerto Rican History

On the other hand, some Puerto Ricans, even if reluctantly admitting the docility charge, have resented what they interpret as Mr. Kazin's denial of Puerto Rican history. These Puerto Ricans, I fear, have gone beyond the actual text of Mr. Kazin's article. His allusions to our historical rootlessness, to our passivity to history, and to the lack of an objective and carefully documented textbook on Puerto Rican history for use in our schools are valid observations that should not be interpreted as a denial of our history, but rather as an open reproach to the system of public education in the colony.

Latin American and European visitors in Puerto Rico are surprised, not to say frankly shocked, by the fact, inconceivable to them, that the average Puerto Rican is so ignorant of and so indifferent and so insensitive to his own past, history, and tradition that he appears (vegetable-like) to be totally lacking in historical consciousness.

Once again, colonial education in Puerto Rico ("progressive" education or whatever term the official pedagogues chose to apply to it) is to blame for this unconsciousness and stupidity of the great majority of the Puerto Rican population today. If, on the one hand, the Puerto Rican child learns the lie that George Washington never told a lie, he very rarely learns—and almost never in the classroom—about the true and important roles played in our history by exemplary figures like Ramón Power, Juan Alejo de Arizmendi, Ramón Emeterio Betances, Ruiz Belvis, Salvador Brau, Rosendo Matienzo Cintrón, or Eugenio María de Hostos, to mention only a few of the many who deserve historical mention.

The Department of Education, almost as an afterthought, sponsors an isolated, timid, and precarious course on Puerto Rican history of only one semester in high school. (The so-called high school is equivalent to the "bachillerato" in Spain in the sense of being pre-college, but it is never equal to it in academic and humanistic preparation.) The Puerto Rican history course does not even have an adequate text. The Department of Education has not conceived, scientifically designed, nor set up, as of now, academic courses on real Puerto Rican history, as opposed to mere propaganda of the colonial party in power or excessive praise of the deformed history of the metropolis.

Puerto Rican educators and North American educators in Puerto Rico conceal their colonial aims behind the so-called doctrine of "progressive education" (originated by Dewey, deformed by Columbia University's Teachers' College, and applied ingenuously to the point of absurdity by candid native pedagogues). As it has been practiced, it is basically antihumanistic, and these educators have succeeded beautifully in increasing to the maximum the unconsciousness, apathy, and even intellectual numbness of the new generations. Its members are made insensitive to their own history, and consequently their self-respect as Puerto Ricans, and, in turn, as human beings, is kept at the lowest possible level.[2]

Who Would Dare to Cast the First Stone?

But even if Mr. Kazin had actually said that Puerto Rico lacks a history of its own (which he did not), who would dare to cast the first stone? Would it be the average young Puerto Rican, who, in his unawareness, has come to believe that he has no past, no tradition, no history? Would it be perhaps, the Puerto Rican colonial politician, who has appointed the colonial educator to do the colonial job? Or would it be the North American who lives here happily without even asking himself where those natives "spring from" whom he observes in passing, but with whom he would never really be disposed to live? Would it be the chancellor of the University of Puerto Rico, Jaime Benítez,[3] who only a few years ago imported from the University of Chicago an impulsive North American historian, ignorant of our language, to have him voice openly, after three short weeks of a tropical vacation in San Juan, Benítez' personal conviction not only that Puerto Rico lacks a history of its own but that there is no such thing as Puerto Rican culture? Who indeed would dare to cast the first stone at Mr. Kazin? Who?

Passing Review

Passing review on the whole affair and its consequences, weighing pros and cons, I am grateful, as a Puerto Rican, to the North American writer Alfred Kazin for the truths in his article. This is not only because of the amusing and revealing sound and fury they provoked locally, but because it is very rare to hear or read a personal report on Puerto Ricans coming from a North American visitor who is neither a public relations official (read political propagandist) on the payroll of the colonial government, nor a hypocritically smiling congressman from Washington, nor an opportunistic New York politician, nor a "good will" visitor on a well-paid vacation in one of our luxury hotels, nor a Point Four "tourist" carefully selected and subsidized by the Department of State in Washington, nor one of those rich young girls, with bourgeois vulgarity and pretentiousness, from Sarah Lawrence, on her offensive annual "poverty vacation" on our island (Go to your own Deep South, young girls!), nor that "generous friend of Puerto Rico" with thousands of dollars invested in the absentee economy of the island for his own profit. We Puerto Ricans are simply fed up with so much hypocritical praise and flattery, so much groveling adulation, so much sugar and honey, so much stupid superficiality, so many polite lies, and so much irritating demagogy, coming from so many "kind," "sincere," "charming," "unconditional," "sweet" *amigos* of Puerto Rico who are showered upon us daily from the skies via the International Airport.

Puerto Rico is engaged today as a people, that is to say, as a national entity, in a mortal struggle for its own survival, even if right now the average Puerto Rican does not realize it. (And when I say *struggle* and *survival* I am certainly not talking about Operation Bootstrap.) Polite words, sweet lies, patronizing attitudes, hypocritical praise, and corrupting flattery is not what Puerto Ricans need in this crucial period.

Mr. Kazin's bitter dosage of truth has been not only refreshing but also healthy for a people he rightly characterizes as docile and bewildered. Granted that docility and bewilderment are common traits of many contemporary Western societies including to a great extent that of the United States (a fact Mr. Kazin failed to mention), they are especially detrimental and self-destructive when deeply rooted in a colonial people. Knowing and facing this fact with fortitude would always be healthier and more patriotic than hypocritically ignoring it.

The Docile Puerto Rican
Literature and Psychological Reality

Definition and Demarcation

Docile, from the latin *docilis,* means "obedient" or "fulfilling the wishes of the one who commands."[1] Sainz de Robles cites, among other synonyms of the word, "meek" and "submissive," which seem to be characteristic of the most generally held meaning. For *docility* (the quality of being docile), the same scholar gives us "subordination," "meekness," "submission."[2]

In Roque Barcia's work we find that the word docility is given a broader range of meaning: "Docility is to lack the strength or even the will to put up resistance to what others demand, insinuate, or command; a propensity to obey, to follow the example, the opinion, the advice of others, which arises either from one's own weakness or failings, or from ignorance, or from lack of confidence in one's own intelligence, knowledge, or strength."[3]

From this definition, we can deduce that the submissive, meek, or docile man is necessarily a weak person ("he lacks the strength or even the will") or an ignorant one ("which arises . . . from ignorance") or the victim of a pathetic inferiority complex ("lack of confidence in one's own intelligence, knowledge, or strength").

Having clarified the term semantically, we propose to prove, throughout this essay, the docility or docile quality of the present-day

Author's note: Essay Prize of the Ateneo Puertorriqueño, 1960. Fragments of the essay were read by the author at the Sixth Congress of Puerto Rican Psychologists, August 26, 1961, at the University of Puerto Rico. The complete text was published in *Cuadernos Americanos* (1962, reprint, 1962); reproduced in the University of Puerto Rico's *Revista de Ciencias Sociales* (1963, reprint, 1963); reprint of the present publication, 1966. The essay now contains appendixes and additional data, written later (1965-66) for its inclusion in this volume.

Puerto Rican. Rather than attempt to discover the reasons for this docility, such as weakness, or ignorance, or complexes, or any intricate combination of these three, our purpose here is to provide the kind of data and analysis which can establish a rational proof of his docility.

Since one may explore the theme in practically any aspect of Puerto Rican society, any point of departure is possible. We have chosen contemporary literature as the springboard for an examination of psychological realities, because the literature amply reflects the diverse phenomena of the society in which it is produced.[4] Presuming that our point of departure is valid, any incident within the social structure can serve as a pretext for approaching it.

The Sound and the Fury of a Psycho-Semantic Problem

When Alfred Kazin, the North American literary critic, irritated the island society with his assertion that the Puerto Rican is docile, the intense guilt complex latent in every colonial society came spectacularly to the surface.[5] Significantly, the reaction of the North American resident in Puerto Rico was much more violent and more virulently verbalized than that of those to whom the commentary referred. The spectacle must have awakened particular interest in two specialized observers of social phenomena: the sociologist and the psychologist.[6] For the nonspecialized observer, the fact that the Puerto Rican victim should be furiously defended by those who—in the technical sense— could be blamed for his plight proved to be either pathetic or amusing, depending on the humor of the spectator.

It is curious that Alfred Kazin, a literary critic, should make such a judgment without having even been acquainted with Puerto Rican literature.[7] This is not to say that our literature exhibits, *prima facie,* characteristics that might justify a theory of docility. The reader often receives the opposite impression from a superficial or frivolous examination of contemporary literature in Puerto Rico. The amount of physical violence it contains would make the uninformed reader think that it is the expression of an aggressive people. There is no doubt, however, that had he been able to read Spanish, Alfred Kazin, an acute critic, would have found his judgment of the Puerto Rican confirmed. He had only to look beyond the surface manifestations of misspent physical energy and violence.

In any event, it is amazing to find that even today the docility of the Puerto Rican is insistently and childishly denied. The problem may be a semantic one. Sociologists, writers, educators, and even so-called "average" citizens have repeated ad nauseam, since the decade of the forties, that the Puerto Rican is *peaceful* and *tolerant*. Previously, he used to be called *fatalistic* and *resigned*. And before that, he had come to be characterized as *aplatanado*[8] and *ñangotado*.[9]

Pedreira was one of those who pointed out our touching weakness for the euphemism, which had been transformed by that time—the decade of the thirties—into the doubtful art of "sugar-coating the pill."[10] Progress, industrialization, and a high standard of living have neither eliminated nor diminished this tendency toward euphemism. Instead, the last thirty years have only intensified it. To see this, one need only look at the words mentioned above in their chronological sequence: the *aplatanado* and *ñangotado* of the twenties, became, in 1930, *resigned* and *fatalistic*; they then evolved with sly hypocrisy into *peaceful* and *tolerant,* the fashionable words today. However, it is the present-day politician in collaboration with an occasional complacent sociologist who has carried the concept to the limit of euphemistic expression: the docile Puerto Rican has come to be, for them, nothing more nor less than *democratic.*

Democracy and *democratic,* terms which are up for grabs, can be used today to adorn almost any concept or situation, in both the Eastern and Western worlds. In Puerto Rico, they are often used by politicians as one more synonym for peaceful, tolerant, resigned, fatalistic, aplatanado, or ñangotado. Thus the Puerto Rican is praised as "democratic" when he tolerates, with asinine docility, what no civilized person would dream of tolerating in any modern democracy. If "aplatanado" was a stinging ethical barb in the stagnant colonial soul, its newest synonym—democratic—is a narcotic drug mercifully administered to quiet the conscience of the docile Puerto Rican so that he may accept, without scruple, his abject condition.

Alfred Kazin's error was to be unaware of this tendency of the present-day Puerto Rican to avoid calling things by their right names— a form of escapism. By using the term *docile* to describe in English a condition which only can be described, with precision, by this term, he forced a pill without sugar-coating into the Puerto Ricans' twisted colonial mechanism. What does the machine of the spirit (or, if one prefers, of the intellect) do when it is forced to stop and consider that what its gears assimilate as peaceful, tolerant, and democratic is nothing but the offensive word, docile? The machine of the intellect (or of the spirit, as one chooses) cannot adjust unexpectedly to assimilate such raw material. It expels the bitter foreign matter with a great grinding of gears—inoffensive belchings of every hypersensitive machine—and resumes the absorption of the usual pills coated with their precious sugar: pacific, tolerant, democratic.

There is no way that the psychosemantic conflict can obscure a fact now known and accepted, under different names and in distinct historic periods, by the subject himself: the Puerto Rican is a docile being.

There is no reason to undertake here an analysis of the causes which have produced such a condition, something already attempted in a commentary on Kazin's article.[11] Of greater importance now is to face the fact itself, independently of its causes, so as to be able to observe its repercussions in some expressions of Puerto Rican life.

The Korean War: Myth or Reality?

Few things are more disturbing than the discussion about Puerto Rican heroism in the Korean War. What disturbs us—we should make clear—is our total ignorance about an experience which has had such important psychological, social, and perhaps even political consequences in Puerto Rican life today. No one in Puerto Rico knows what happened in Korea to the Puerto Ricans, or putting it in another way, what happened to the Puerto Ricans in the North American army in Korea. The white paper (or the blue, red, or black) on that historic episode from the Puerto Rican point of view has not been written. Sociologists, historians, and psychologists have ignored the war as a collective Puerto Rican phenomenon. The few available statistics could perhaps give us exact figures on this or that, but they reveal nothing about the fundamental facts. What happened in Korea? What was the attitude of the "average" Puerto Rican toward his war experience? What was his reaction to the *issue* involved; to the army he was a part of; to the citizenship for which he was contributing, without representation, his own blood; to the Korean people for whose presumed liberty he was fighting? Why was there such a high proportion of the mentally unbalanced—to use one more euphemism—among our Korean veterans? What was the consensus of the North American officers about their Puerto Rican soldiers? And that of the Puerto Rican soldiers about their North American officers? Why did the Korean War cause the permanent dissolution of the 65th Infantry Regiment, until then and for many years the only unit in the North American Army composed entirely of Puerto Ricans?

Until a thorough investigation can give us reliable answers to these questions, we will continue to find disturbing the fact that some Puerto Ricans, the majority of them now dead, mutilated, or psychopathic, received, as individuals, medals in the Korean conflict; we are even more disturbed by the monumental ignorance—better yet, tremendous indifference—of our social scientists concerning the collective phenomenon of the Puerto Rican in Korea.

Since the social sciences have shed no light on the question, we must turn to literature for a glimpse of facts which could only be documented by certain papers buried in some United States Army files in Washington, if they still exist. Fortunately, a young writer, Emilio Díaz Valcárcel, a Korean veteran, has recreated the collective experience in several of his short stories. "El Soldado Damián Sánchez,"[12] a good example of his treatment of the theme, reflects, not the myth of heroism, but the psychology of the weak and docile man, the perfect antihero. The protagonist, part of a military unit composed mainly of North Americans, has as his only friend a South Korean soldier, perhaps because he has found in him affinities to his own condition as a Puerto Rican. But Damián finds himself trapped to the point of exasperation by the prejudices, abuses, and injustices he suffers at the hands of his North American companions and officers. Instead of reacting against them, he relieves his fury, in a seemingly illogical way, by unjustly, viciously, and cruelly beating up his Korean friend, the only person who, at that moment, he can consider weaker or "inferior."

The psychological mechanism of a weak and docile man has seldom been dramatized so acutely and so accurately. The story gives us the key to why a "peaceful" and "tolerant" society like the Puerto Rican can produce a literature of violence. The violent acts of literary characters—and these abound in all the prose genres—are not, in the last analysis, the product of a revolutionary doctrine, of a heroic tradition, of a conscious and shining defiance, or of a normal and healthy aggression. Rather these acts arise from the desperation of weak and docile beings cornered in the last redoubt of human dignity.

The Nationalist movement inspired several works which better illustrate this kind of behavior. The protagonist of the short story "La muerte" does not take a stand, in the political-heroic sense, on the Ponce Massacre.[13] He accepts the fact of death as an existential solution, and his action, judged by common standards, could be called passive. Michel Lefranc, ex-university professor in the play by the same author, *Un niño azul para esa sombra,* is only a weak if not docile intellectual whom direct action—the one and only aggressive gesture in his life—leads to destruction. An exception to this rule of violence arising from exasperation is the short story, "El juramento," in which the docile personality of the Puerto Rican is carried to its furthest and most absurd consequences.[14] Here the violence of which the character is a victim does not provoke any aggressive action on his part. The protagonist—significantly unnamed—is not even a Nationalist. An innocent bystander, he nonetheless becomes a victim of the official version of the 1950 revolt and of the McCarthian juridical doctrine of "guilt by association." Once trapped within the implacable mechanism of the state which devours him, he remains inert, accepting his situation with characteristic fatalism. He observes with cynical lucidity all the absurd details of the process which crushes him, incapable, nevertheless, of any initiative which might help to alter the course of his destiny. Aside from the fact that the author might have intended to dramatize or symbolize a universal problem of contemporary man, the psychology of the character and the social, political, and juridical details which set that psychology in motion are authentically Puerto Rican. Their verisimilitude only becomes clear upon studying the Puerto Rican within the context of his cultural environment at a specific moment in time.

Nationalism and Annexationism: The Self-Destructive Impulse

In real life and in literature the Nationalist phenomenon dramatizes another psycho-social problem: the Puerto Rican's notorious self-destructive impulse, his suicidal tendency. Is repressing or inhibiting the normal aggressive impulse so as to direct it morbidly toward oneself a characteristic of docile people and nations (read ñangotados, tolerant, democratic)? The matter is perhaps debatable, but until an authority on psychology proves the contrary, we can accept it as a characteristic of the psychological picture of docility.

The literature of the last twenty years in Puerto Rico contains, as has been recently noted, an alarming number of suicides, either literal or potential.[15] It might be said that the phenomenon is a feature of contemporary Western literature. But there is an interesting statistic which can explain the fact within the island limits: Puerto Rico has the highest suicide rate of any Catholic country in the world.[16]

The Third Theater Festival (1960), aside from its possible dramatic merits, did reflect this circumstance, giving us at least one suicide in five of the six works presented. Earlier, the three local dramas most warmly received by the public during the last twenty years — *Tiempo Muerto, La Carreta,* and *Los Soles Truncos* — dramatized the suicidal tendency without any ambiguity. In the narrative genres, our most brilliant short story writers of the moment — José Luis González, Abelardo Díaz Alfaro, Pedro Juan Soto, and Emilio Díaz Valcárcel, among others — without even touching the Nationalist phenomenon, emphasize the suicidal impulse of the Puerto Rican. *Spiks,* a collection of stories about Puerto Ricans in New York, and *El asedio* are typical.[17]

Puerto Rican Nationalism undoubtedly reveals the suicidal psychology most clearly. One need only glance at the violence of the Nationalists in the last thirty years. Except for the political assassination of

Col. Riggs—the only time when they achieved their immediate objective—the Nationalists' assaults have resulted in a series of spectacular failures. What psychological flaw has made these patriotic, determined, and bold armed men fail in each one of their many attempts at political terrorism? The key must lie in the irrational suicidal impulse that dragged them into action. The real objective was not to kill or, even less, to achieve victory, but to die. Besides obvious cases like the Ponce Massacre, the assault on Blair House in Washington can be seen as clearly suicidal, not because of the objective certainly, nor even because of the risks involved, but because of the way in which the Nationalists tried to reach their objective. True revolutionaries, bold but politically disciplined within a freedom-seeking movement, or professionals in political terrorism, ready to risk their lives but without the obsession or the resolute purpose of dying, would probably have achieved what turned out to be impossible for the Puerto Rican Nationalists.

Perhaps we should conclude that the cohesiveness of the Nationalist movement in its years of greatest activity was based more on a psychological condition common to its members—the suicidal impulse of the Puerto Rican carried to its greatest extreme—than on a revolutionary doctrine or on a terrorist methodology. Indeed, the Nationalist movement had no methodology. Compare the planned, methodical, and effective political terrorism of the Algerian underground or of the Cypriot liberation movement—target chosen, target hit—with the erratic terrorism, unmethodical and useless—suicidal, in short—of Puerto Rican Nationalism.[18]

The Nationalist suicidal impulse, which could be described by the euphemism "martyr complex," appears in various literary works. The theme is introduced for the first time in the short story which gives its title to the already mentioned volume *Otro Dia Nuestro* (1955), and it is repeated successively, in the theater, with *Palm Sunday* (1956) by René Marqués, *Encrucijada* (1958) by Manuel Méndez Ballester, *El Final de la Calle* (1959) by Gerard Paul Marín, and *Un niño Azul Para Esa Sombra* (1960) by René Marqués; in the novel, with *La Ceiba en el Tiesto* (1956) by Enrique A. Laguerre, *Los Derrotados* (1957) by César Andreu Iglesias, and *El Gigante y el Alba* (1959) by Ricardo Cordero.[19]

But the Nationalists [20] are not the only ones in the contemporary Puerto Rican political arena who dramatize the self-destructive impulse. Certainly their case is the more spectacular one since it involves physical suicide. Nevertheless, on the opposite extreme, the assimilationists, the Commonwealth partisans, and the annexationists reveal clear suicidal symptoms in varying degrees. With them, however, the irrepressible impulse toward self-destruction manifests itself not on the physical but on the moral and spiritual planes. It we take, as a pretext, two opposing ideologies, the Nationalist and the annexationist, we will find that they coincide in their urgent desire for self-destruction. The gesture of the Nationalist who attacks Blair House in search of death is as suicidal as that of the annexationist who attacks his own Puerto Rican essence in search of a moral and spiritual death. Ideologically, they appear as opposites, but psychologically they are kindred Puerto Rican souls.

There is a difference between them. The Nationalist almost always literally accomplishes his purpose: he dies violently. The annexationist, on the other hand, is a living dead man, a never completely realized suicide, a man self-condemned to destroy himself slowly as a Puerto Rican without ever achieving his goal. He cannot totally destroy his Puerto Rican being while he still lives and breathes. The annexationist's pathetic state of eternal self-condemnation explains the degree of self-betrayal, humiliation, and servility which he can on occasion achieve in his suicidal determination to annul or destroy his Puerto Rican personality.

The phenomenon reaches its highest level of absurdity in the black annexationist. Born in a culture where racial prejudice has been kept, in this century of bloody conflicts, at a very low level, he struggles desperately and suicidally to destroy those cultural patterns of human sociability in order to merge his country into a foreign culture where prejudice against the black reaches levels of hate, cruelty, and savagery never experienced in contemporary Puerto Rican society.

Significantly, among the founders of Puerto Rican annexationism at the beginning of the century, there were several blacks who were intelligent, cultured, and proud, moreover, of their race and of their condition as Puerto Ricans. This makes the paradox even more dramatic.[21] Significantly, also, it can be stated with certainty that most blacks in Puerto Rico are annexationists. There is no doubt that in the black Puerto Rican the suicidal impulse is more acute than in the white, since today annexationism means for him an even greater degree of self-destruction than physical death signifies for the white.

How can one explain such a complex paradox? Or would it be more appropriate to ask: what psychological mechanism has the black Puerto Rican annexationist developed to reconcile his inescapable racial condition with his suicidal political ideology? The mechanism is simple and it is not, certainly, peculiar to the black, but functions equally well in the white Puerto Rican. In the former, however, the phenomenon is most obvious, which makes analysis easier.

This mechanism consists of the atrophying of the rational power of association in certain zones of the intellect. There develops a comfortable and convenient incapacity to associate or relate intellectually certain situations, facts, and ideas. It is in this way that the black annexationist lets the tragedy of Little Rock slide off his dark skin, as well as the lynchings of blacks in the South, and the racial war in certain sectors of New York and Chicago without associating, even remotely, these sociopolitical expressions of the culture of the United States with his condition as a black Puerto Rican who aspires to become a black North American.

We repeat, nevertheless, that the strange phenomenon is not peculiar to the black annexationist. The "average" Puerto Rican, whatever his race, can read a novel, see a movie, or follow a television series whose theme may be the struggle for the freedom of a country which is or was colonial (Ireland, Cyprus, Cuba, Poland, Algeria, or the thirteen American colonies, for example) without it occurring to him, even remotely, to relate what he reads, sees, or hears to the colonial condition of his own country.

It would be an error to believe that this psychological blindness afflicts the "average" citizen exclusively. Most Popular Democratic or Commonwealth intellectuals in Puerto Rico contemptuously characterize the concepts of country and freedom as *obsolete,* the believers in national sovereignty as *deluded* and *crazy,* the Nationalists as *assassins,* and as *romantics* those who place the dignity of man on a higher lever than the mere digestive process. These are the same intellectuals who publicly, joyously, and noisily supported Fidel Castro and his 26th of July movement. They never stopped to observe that those revolutionary peasants were obsolete, deluded, crazy, nationalists, assassins, and romantics, in precisely the way they—the believers in the Commonwealth—had used the terms. Thanks to the mechanism we are speaking of, the Popular Democractic intellectuals could fervidly praise in Cuba what they condemned with equal fervor in Puerto Rico without being at all conscious of the flagrant contradiction in their attitude.[22] This psychological block, this notorious incapacity to associate situations, facts, and ideas intellectually, should now be considered typical of the Puerto Rican personality.

Literature spreads a strange veil of silence over the annexationist phenomenon itself. It could be argued that this is because Puerto Rican writers uphold—almost to a man—the ideal of independence or, said in another way, because virtually no Puerto Rican citizen deserving the name of writer is annexationist. The argument is perhaps valid, but it is still a little superficial. Nothing would prevent the pro-independence writer from touching on the annexationist phenomenon in order to condemn it in his work. Why, then, doesn't he do it? It is impossible to argue that the theme is not literary material since the Puerto Rican annexationist, as a human being, is a tremendously pathetic character, capable, therefore, of being transformed into a literary creation.

It seems that it is not political prejudice on the part of the creator nor the sterility of the raw material which causes the inhibition, but an ethical problem. The theme provokes a strange sensation of shyness in the writer. It is as if he felt that annexationism would contaminate his writing. Writers who have handled the most risqué themes skillfully and boldly, and who have probed with cruel objectivity, and without scruple, the miseries of the Puerto Rican and his society, hold back from the annexationist theme with something very akin to repugnance. They do not even deem it worthy of attack. The ethical man's sacred horror of such a doctrine, although comprehensible in many ways, is creating a gap in contemporary Puerto Rican literature which must be filled. The mission of the writer is always that of revealing, clarifying, and illuminating. No phenomenon is so in need of revelation, clarification, and illumination for the benefit of the very slightly illuminated Puerto Rican as the psychological phenomenon of annexationism. The writer should never refuse to pick up the glove which reality, in a mocking gesture, throws at this feet.[23]

Synthesis of Puerto Rican Psychology: The Commonwealth Ideal

The two extreme phenomena—Nationalism and annexationism—which we have examined in the political field, have somewhat complex psychological mechanisms. Nevertheless, it is in the middle road, that of the Commonwealth, that Puerto Rican docility finds its most comfortable and natural expression, free of psychological complications. This political monster strikes us as brilliant, not for the reasons given by its eulogizers, but because it has been able, in an almost doctrinaire fashion, to mimic the psychological make-up of the people who are its raison d'être. The Commonwealth is, in fact, the authentic expression of compromise, the embodiment of euphemism, the finished product of the spurious art of sugar-coating the pill; in other words, it is the psychological synthesis of the weak, timid, and docile man.

Those who accuse its supposed creator[24] of having an Anglo-Saxon mentality do not seem to understand that only an authentic docile Puerto Rican could accommodate in a single political formula the most keenly felt psychological vices of the Puerto Rican. When the present supporter of the formula affirms, for demagogical ends, that the Commonwealth is not his creation, but that of the Puerto Rican people, he is more correct than he himself, honorably, would want to admit. On the other hand, when the Commonwealth adherents declare that this formula reflects the inescapable economic reality of Puerto Rico, they are simply rationalizing a more inescapable, authentic, and determining reality: the psychological one. The elevation of his docility to the rank of political dogma was precisely what the Puerto Rican needed to exist spiritually and morally within his traditional ñangotamiento[25] without remorse or scruples of conscience.

The Commonwealth itself, as a political doctrine, has scarcely had a place in Puerto Rican literature. The only panegyrist of the colonial status quo has been José A. Balseiro, in his novel *En Vela Mientras el Mundo Duerme*.[26] Although it does not amount to an apologia, Enrique A. Laguerre also reveals certain Commonwealth-oriented postures or attitudes in some passages of *La Ceiba en el Tiesto*.[27]

On the other hand, it is not necessary for the Puerto Rican writer to focus directly on the Commonwealth in order to express its political and ethical nature. Almost all Puerto Rican literature of recent years—even that prior to 1952, the year of the latest colonial reforms—has an admonitory tone which is usually accusing and often prophetic in its comments on the present political system. In this sense it can be said that Puerto Rican literature during the last two decades—before and after the Commonwealth—has been fundamentally anti-Commonwealth. This is understandable, since the writer—rebel without a cause—will never be able to conciliate, in Puerto Rico or in any other society of the civilized world, his ethical concept of freedom and human dignity with the anti-ethical reality of colonialism under whatever name or circumstances it may be produced.

The Authoritarian Cultural Pattern

If one undertakes a superficial examination of the world of Puerto Rican officialdom, one will soon see that beneath the epithet of "democratic" a gigantic political machine functions, docilely, without any difficulty, run entirely according to an authoritarian pattern. When our social scientist is forced to perceive the anomaly of the situation, he uses the euphemism "paternalism" to describe it. (The occasions in which he has the capacity, will, and courage to perceive it are apparently not very frequent, since he rarely informs us of it.)

Paternal or authoritarian—that, in the last analysis, is the psychosocial pattern which prevails in Puerto Rico's apparently democratic society. This fact is the daily bread of our public life, and it would be pointless to attempt a list of examples. It is enough to mention the absolute and infantile dependence of the Puerto Rican legislature on the executive power, a psychological and cultural fact which mocks in a tropical fashion the wise and serious constitutional postulates imported from other climes and other psychologies.

But whoever thinks that authoritarianism is limited to the career-politician mentality in the government ought to turn his eyes to a supposedly more intellectual and cultured environment: the University of Puerto Rico. He will note the strange submission of the faculty to the authoritarian patterns imposed by the administration in spite of the recently established and so widely proclaimed Academic Senate. In this case a curious factor intervenes which serves to reinforce Puerto Rican docility: the total identification of most of the European and South and North American professors—a large group at present—with the authoritarian politics of the administration. This is a comprehensible reaction given the sense of insecurity which the foreigner experiences on finding himself unexpectedly thrust into a cultural structure strange to him and even, perhaps, hostile, depending on his own complexes and resentments as an exile.[28]

The authoritarian pattern is not exclusive to official spheres; it permeates all groups in Puerto Rican society. In political parties, labor unions and syndicates, professional associations, civil organizations, and cultural institutions, power tends to be concentrated and perpetuated, often in one person. The democratic process, followed externally and mechanically—with meticulous and pathetic scrupulosity on occasion—is only a polite fiction to hide the real situation: unmitigated authoritarianism. Thus it is not rare to see puppet directors and presidents in organizations in which the dictator, with sly hypocrisy, finds it expedient to hide his power "behind the throne." A de jure democracy and a de facto authoritarian government—this is an exact description not only of the Puerto Rican state but of all those groups organized more or less on the margin of direct political influence.[29]

The authoritarian pattern, in a good number of its expressions or manifestations, appears directly or indirectly, consciously or unconsciously, in almost all our contemporary literature. The short stories of Miguel Meléndez Muñoz, Emilio S. Belaval, Abelardo Díaz Alfaro, and José Luis González emphasize the theme. It concerned Laguerre in several of his novels, and especially in *La Llamarada*, Méndez Ballester in one of his first dramas, *Tiempo Muerto*, Pedro Juan Soto in his recent *Usmail*, and René Marqués in *La Muerte No Entraʐa en*

Palacio, this last a tragedy where the problem is explored directly in its current manifestation: de facto authoritarianism masked by a de jure democracy.[30]

The Matriarchal Pattern

Within the psychological panorama of Puerto Rican docility, the literature of the last twenty years reveals something of inescapable importance: the sudden appearance of women as leading characters in literary works. One author has already pointed out that it is the younger writers "who have achieved feminine characterizations of greater tragic heights and of deeper psychological penetration."[31] Some might ask what relation there is between well-developed feminine characters and Puerto Rican docility, arguing that in any case the only thing this shows is a greater degree of maturity in our literature, since the bulk of the best Western literature from Euripides down to the present has been achieved principally through female characters. As well as being flattering to our present literature, this observation is a valid one, as long as it is taken as a very general rule with not infrequent and notable exceptions. In accepting it as a sign of maturity, we would agree that a man of letters only obtains his "doctorate" as a writer when his analytical capacity enables him to explore objectively the psychological world of the opposite sex—an evasive, mysterious, and for him undoubtedly, poor devil, very dangerous world. But as flattering as the general or universal explanation may be, it is not, to our mind, a determining factor, though it might be a secondary one.

It seems likely that the literary fact is the result of a Puerto Rican social phenomenon: the introduction of the Anglo-Saxon-style matriarchal pattern in 1940 and its consistent and devastating development in the course of the last twenty years. Before this period the cultural pattern of paterfamilias prevailed, though our women did enjoy those legal rights to which they had laid claim, and one could find in Puerto Rican literature, after a tiresome search, only a few feminine characterizations of appreciable merit. This is not the case in the literatures of contemporary societies where the paterfamilias pattern still prevails (the French, Spanish, or Italian, for example), for they offer a wealth of female literary characters of the first rank.

Naturally, when we speak of the frequency of good female characterizations in our contemporary literature, we refer to psychological and esthetic attainments and not to any moral value. To tell the truth, the young writers seem to take a savage revenge on matriarchy—a foreign pattern recently imported into their culture—by often presenting women in the worst possible light. Apparently, the writers are the only ones in Puerto Rican society who have aggressively rebelled against the disappearance of the last cultural bulwark from which one could still combat, in part, the collective docility: *machismo,* the creole version of the fusion and adaptation of two secular concepts, Spanish *honor* and the Roman paterfamilias.

It would be difficult to present in detail the actual threat posed by the matriarchal system in Puerto Rico, because of the lack not of proof but of space. For each case of fossilized *machismo* which the social worker manages to find in a remote mountain field or in some not completely Americanized district of the city, we are sure that we can show her—if her superior, the female sociologist, provides us with the proper research tools—two or more cases of flagrant matriarchal transgression in the always growing and mighty middle class. This is the social stratum responsible for the introduction of cultural patterns in a mesocratic society, which is what ours is rapidly becoming. One might add that a glance at present-day Puerto Rican public life gives the measure of the docility of the ex-paterfamilias, who presents a sad figure when faced with the aggressive advance of woman in all the spheres in which he was once, in a nostalgic past, lord and master. It is scant consolation for the native anthropologist to observe how one of the traits of Puerto Rican docility passes, unaltered, from the hands of the woman to those of the man.

Let us leave, in our turn, in the hands of the psychologist or, better yet, of the psychiatrist, the prediction as to what this new cultural reality signifies for the future Puerto Rican society. We are satisfied for the moment to refer the sociologist—who at the present could still be either male or female—to the recent population census, which yields in certain geographic sectors an alarming imbalance in the proportion of the sexes, due, it is alleged, to the masculine emigration to the United States. Political, social, cultural, economic, and psychological factors seem to coincide in the rapid solidifying of a matriarchal pattern in Puerto Rican society. As far as we know —and our information could be deficient—the credit for having given the first voice of frank alarm with respect to a problem which should be the direct incumbency of anthropologists, sociologists, and psychologists goes to the literary symbol.[32]

Civism and Religion: Social Imposition of English[33]

A transverse cross section (even a partial one) of collective attitudes and modes of expression would necessarily reveal areas untouched by our writers. Some of these are significant if we are to obtain a clearer perspective on the national psychology.

In the following pages, given the impossibility of direct literary references, and so as to sustain the thematic unity announced in our subtitle—literature and psychological reality—we are going to permit ourselves, when we judge it opportune, to fill the literary vacuum by creating a little literature ourselves. The prudent reader, we are sure, will not let himself be thrown off the track by one or two touches of humor or flights of fancy, to the point of losing sight of the real analysis slightly concealed behind the mask of Dionysus.

Without more preamble, let us introduce the theme with one of those anecdotes which North Americans so like to cultivate in their sentimental and optimistic magazines of the style of the *Readers' Digest:* A Puerto Rican writer was recently invited to speak at the Rotary Club of San Juan. What he spoke about does not matter, but since some ill-disposed person might think that the writer presented himself to the honorable members of International Rotarianism to inform them of something of fundamental interest to their membership—industrial development, for example, or methods to increase sales in ten lessons, perhaps—we must make clear that his talk of ten minutes dealt, modestly, with Puerto Rican theater and was motivated by the San Juan Drama Festival's announcement of their intention to put on a Puerto Rican work in English translation.

It was no surprise to the invited writer, nor would it be to anyone, that the Rotary Club of San Juan speaks English exclusively, both in its formal ceremonies and in its regular meetings and deliberations. This is natural—natural in our social environment, that is—since the president of the Club is North American and the membership includes a respectable number of industrialists, bankers, and businessmen who are not only North American, but also mostly monolingual. As a guest, nevertheless, the writer felt free to communicate his ideas in the language of his preference, choosing naturally the one which he had absorbed with pleasure from his mother as a child.

It is not exactly to the point, but it seems fair to make it clear as a tribute to the high degree of democratic courtesy shown by that civic group, that the individual and collective attitude was irreproachable. This violation of the linguistic dogma did not cause any disagreeable incidents. No one, it is also fair to say, accused the guest of being intellectually incompetent for having spoken, before a mixed audience, in his own language. On the contrary, the majority of the North American faces showed an expression of concentration and genuine interest as if it were important for them to try to understand what was being said in Spanish. The writer spoke, it goes without saying, slowly and correctly.

The talk and applause over, a middle-aged North American stood up and asked the president for permission to speak, after which he exclaimed in his own language: "I thank heavens that for the first time I have heard good Spanish spoken in the Rotary Club of San Juan!" The brief speech of the gentleman from North America was received with heavy and sustained applause.

Discounting the element of humor that the incident may contain, we find two points to be interesting and revealing: that it was a North American who, in the Rotary Club of Puerto Rico, expressed a veiled reproach of the linguistic policy of the civic organization to which he belonged, and that most of those who warmly applauded that reproach were Puerto Rican. We suspect that no Puerto Rican present would have said in public what the North American said. But we also suspect, to judge by the applause, that a good number of Puerto Ricans felt an underlying sense of guilt about the problem.

The language battle in local civic organizations is not always won by English, however. Very recently, another men's civic club in the metropolitan area denied the motion of one of its members to make it a bilingual organization, that is to say, to utilize English and Spanish indiscriminantly in its meetings. The proposal was defeated, by an overwhelming majority, with the official use of Spanish being conserved, except for the routine oath of allegiance to the North American flag.[34] The proposer of the motion, a Puerto Rican annexationist, indignant at and humiliated by his defeat, resigned. We do not know exactly what factors caused the triumph of the vernacular in this isolated case except, perhaps, the fact that there are only three North American members and all three—an extraordinary phenomenon—speak Spanish. This nullified the usual argument that Puerto Rican groups in which there are North American members should officially adopt English "as a courtesy." Another important factor is without a doubt a political one (the party affiliation of the majority of the membership), and this we do not know. Yet another contributing factor might be that, in this case, the club was situated on the outskirts of the city, and was smaller, more intimate, and more "provincial" than those in the center of San Juan, and in all probability more social than mercantile in character. One must take into account, nevertheless, that this area will soon undergo intensive industrial development. One can predict that, within a couple of years, English will replace Spanish even here. A motion recognizing the wisdom of the motion defeated today will be approved unanimously tomorrow and the humiliated annexationist will return triumphant to the collective bosom. His Puerto Rican companions will rise to their feet, receive him with smiles and a wave of the hand, and shout in unison: "Hi, Joe!"[35]

Having examined the problem in the civic field, let us cast a glance at the religious area. Among the diverse religious groups, it is the Catholic Church which shows the greatest persistence in imposing the social use of English.[36] With the encouragement of Monsignor James P. Davis, the present Archbishop of Puerto Rico, certain practices have become common now in the metropolitan area which are not only new but also foreign to Puerto Rican secular Catholicism. Sheets circulate, for example, with the imperious command: *Retire in English.* This does not refer, of course, as a native monolinguist might think with exemplary candor, to Federal Social Security, but, simply, to going into a Spiritual Retreat in English.[37] Similarly, the Church, the guardian in every Catholic country of the secular culture, encourages confession in English in presumably "sophisticated" circles of "nouveaux americains" in Puerto Rico. Adjusting to Monsignor Davis' policy, various organizations have made praiseworthy efforts to follow the latest linguistic-religious fashion. One organization of Catholic men—a type of celestial Elks because of their advanced state of North Americanization—does everything in English: invitations, telephone calls, meetings, deliberations, confessions,and retreats. If the impartial observer did not have his sense of humor somewhat dulled, he might perhaps think that the practitioners of the new Catholicism in Puerto Rico cherish the mystic hope of a moving scene: Saint Peter opening for them the gates of Heaven to the chords of the Star Spangled Banner. (A hope, we admit, which is as Christianly pious as any other that might lack celestial stereophonic sound.)

The social imposition of English, however, is not limited to civic organizations and the Catholic Church. In the School of Medicine they courteously ask the students if they wish the class in English or in Spanish. Only one need prefer it in English for the course to be taught in that language during the whole academic year. The rest of the Puerto Rican students—an absolute majority minus one—do not dare to make the slightest protest, which shows how linguistic democracy is faring in those surroundings. The picture is more or less the same in a good number of the other colleges and departments of the University.[38] Nevertheless, we will call a halt here and enter no further into the turbid field of pedagogy.[39]

Leaving religion and pedagogy aside, no one in today's world can blind himself to the reality that English is in our times the business language par excellence, as were Greek, Latin, Portuguese, French, and Spanish in different historical epochs, and perhaps as Russian may be destined to become in the future. Since the United States is still the dominating economic power in the West, the small world of commerce and banking operates and communicates in the imperial language. This is a general phenomenon which should cause no special alarm in a normally constituted society with a well-defined personality.

Nevertheless, when a colonial society of a distinct language and culture imposes English upon itself, not only as a strict necessity in the business sector, but as a political and cultural instrument disguised as a "social fashion," in order to supplant the vernacular and with it the still prevalent values of the autochthonous culture, it is worth the trouble to explore the psychological roots of the phenomenon.

It will not have escaped the notice of the objective observer that today in Puerto Rico it is not the state which officially imposes the foreign language, although it does encourage it in an undercover manner. The imposition of English is principally in the hands of a series of extra-official Puerto Rican groups—professional, civic, and religious. We should consider the psychological implications of this social regimentation practiced by the upper strata of Puerto Rican society.

The motivations behind such a "fashion" must be very powerful, since the imposition itself constitutes a sacrifice for the Puerto Rican. The use of a foreign language always implies an additional intellectual effort and a tension not normal in a conversation in one's native tongue. It places the person whose language is not being spoken at an intellectual or psychological disadvantage. In addition, in this case the foreign language is fraught with mental burdens, ambivalencies, and psychological conflicts: colony-colonial power, Puerto Rican-North American, inferior-superior, weak-strong, docile-aggressive. Thus, even without his perceiving it, the Puerto Rican will experience extraordinary mental and emotional fatigue.

It is always interesting in Puerto Rico to observe a Puerto Rican and a North American communicating with each other when a business transaction is not involved. When it is, the North American's business sense may force him to use the typical salesman's approach of psychological concessions and flattery toward his client which necessarily conceal the latter's inferior position from the eyes of the casual observer. In other circumstances, however, when the conversation is not directly related to the economic advantages which the North American hopes to gain, the respective national guilt complexes come to the surface in one way or another.

The North American in Puerto Rico feels himself guilty, although never consciously, of imperialism. This guilt is translated into one of two extreme attitudes. He may exhibit the aggressive arrogance of the "superior" man who must prove to himself the validity and morality of his position, saying, in effect: "I am an imperialist because, after all, I *am* superior". On the other hand, he may become benevolently condescending in his desire to prove *to others* the legitimacy and advantages of the imperialist policy. This consists of a humanitarian concern to help the weak or "inferior" person. (He cannot, of course, be helped a lot, because this would endanger the imperialist's insecure position of "superiority"). The North American himself has called this spiritual posturing a "patronizing attitude" (while in Spanish we would call it, with greater accuracy than the term might reveal at first glance, an "attitude of patronal benevolence").

It seems opportune to point out in this respect that so-called North American humanitarianism operates almost always on the material or economic plane, very rarely on the ethical or spiritual one. A study of the process of contemporary North American Caesarism brings one to the conclusion that the North American has restricted the term freedom to a narrow economic definition: freedom from hunger.[40] In practice, this freedom can be condensed in an axiom: the nation which buys what it consumes in the United States market is "free" and "democratic." If it occurs to one of the nations under North American tutelage—and it does not have to be literally a colony like Puerto Rico—to carry the term freedom to the spiritual and ethical plane, alleging either that man does not live by bread alone or that the most tasty or most worthy bread is one's own although it may be less soft and less white, North American "humanitarianism" feels wounded to the core. The power of the empire moves diligently to crush that nation which dared to violate the North American dogma of "freedom." (In this respect, Cuba and Puerto Rico may not be "of one bird, two wings,"[41] but they have certainly been two very similar feathers in the ostentatious plumage of the same imperial bird.) We have, then, to realize that United States "humanitarianism" is to a great extent nothing but a rationalization of the peremptory necessities of its economic empire. Each country "freed" from hunger by the United States becomes a captive market within the complex North American economic network. Any attempt by that country to overstep the bounds in its attainment of freedom (most especially national economic freedom) constitutes a grave offense against "democracy," that is, against the United States' imperial economy. It will have to pay for this offense, if it is in the United States' power to make it do so. The punishment will be economic aggression, or a hunger seige, from which it will again be "freed" once it accepts the conditions of North American "humanitarianism" which it before had the audacity to refuse.

All of this, which is very tragic, and very real for the parties involved, forms an unexamined and unreasoned psychological sediment in the mind of the North American in Puerto Rico. Such conflicts and ambivalences become conscious material only for those North Americans who possess a great deal of sensitivity as well as culture. There are, naturally, very few of these in Puerto Rico. It is in them, nevertheless, that one can best observe all the complexities of the North American psychology. There is an undercurrent of anguish in their dealings with Puerto Ricans. The urgency to belong causes them to make a sincere and honest effort to understand the Puerto Rican and sympathize with his idiosyncrasies and his cultural patterns. But they never accomplish this completely, perhaps because their uneasiness over their "betrayal" of North American values disturbs them too much. Black sheep among the North American residents, they cannot help but see themselves as "ugly ducklings" in the Puerto Rican social group.Some, unable to stand the external tensions, arrive at the illusory compromise of pretending to be, simultaneously, North Americans among the North American residents and Puerto Ricans among the Puerto Ricans. Such psychological acrobatics in the long run cause their moral, spiritual, and intellectual deterioration. (Their sociologists and psychologists then cite the enervating tropical climate as the cause of this deterioration.)

On confronting the North American, the Puerto Rican for his part sets in motion his colonial guilt complex.[42] In order to tolerate his humiliating condition he has to find an excuse for it and admit that he is *inferior* to the North American. This motivates his obsequiousness (the traditional "courtesy," "hospitality," and "generosity") expressed in ways which closely approach servility. This unconscious admission of inferiority cannot help but hurt his ego, often provoking extreme compensatory reactions such as violent antagonism or total surrender. The most interesting from the psychological point of view is, without doubt, the latter, since by surrendering he is able to dispense with his defense mechanisms and open himself up, without resistance, to all that is North American. He hopes in this way to acquire or to incorporate the "superiority" of that feared and envied being, but, of course, he never can. In many Puerto Ricans who have some sensitivity as well as education and culture, these extreme manifestations never appear in all their brutal clarity. They develop a strange ambivalence in their social dealings with the North American, similar, in its undercurrent of anguish, to that of the sensitive North American when he tries to fraternize with the Puerto Rican.

Only in authentically bilingual individuals who believe they have resolved their ambivalence toward the politico-cultural problem into which they were born—and in Puerto Rico there are scarcely a handful of these tropical icebergs—can the painful defense mechanism be reduced to a minimum. When they communicate with a North American there appear to be no barriers. The few Puerto Ricans who, because they were raised or educated in the United States, speak English fluently but Spanish less so, are not true bilingual speakers. With them the mechanism functions inversely: they are made uneasy by Spanish. This is aggravated by the fact that, forced to use the native tongue of their compatriots in their communication with other Puerto Ricans, they develop an additional guilt complex precisely because they cannot handle it perfectly. So they avoid it, using it as little as possible. They then advocate English as the "official" language in the circles in which they move or they retire to narrow little social islands—no man's lands—where other cultural pariahs like themselves have already imposed the use of the foreign tongue.

It is becoming clear that English in Puerto Rico is not simply another foreign language, like French or Italian, but the painful site of many conflicting experiences—political, cultural, spiritual, and psychological —which exacerbate the Puerto Rican's colonial anguish.

The imposition and social acceptance of English in Puerto Rico can be viewed, then, without risk of error, as one more manifestation of Puerto Rican docility.

Scientific Objectivity and State Control

Let us now turn toward another aspect of the Puerto Rican personality, exemplified in the attitude of some social scientists. [43]The euphemism, the circumlocution, and the sugar-coating of the pill characteristic of this psychology find a comfortable refuge in so-called "scientific objectivity." These professionals conveniently develop such scientific scrupulosity that it paralyzes their understanding. In their studies in the social sciences, which follow a rigorous and arduous methodology, nothing is ever said, or, at any rate, so little is said and so blandly that it is not worth the money, work, and time invested. The same thing could have been deduced at first glance and with more certainty without recourse to such complicated scientific procedures. They are, certainly, excellent in research, since their docility enables them conscientiously to carry out the whole vexatious procedure imposed by the methodology. But when the moment arrives for analysis, for interpretation, and for coming to conclusions in accordance with their data, they often have to depend on another usually imported expert to examine the results and arrive at conclusions.

Even in cases in which this type of Puerto Rican specialist decides to make or is told to make his own interpretations, his conclusions frequently show a tact which reflects, not scientific accuracy, but rather timidity: an infantile fear of committing himself, a childish apprehension about having and upholding, as a scientist, his own criteria.

Lack of professional initiative and of creative originality are also typical. The Puerto Rican specialist passively waits for the imported expert to indicate what field should be explored. It seldom occurs to him—and when it does he rarely exerts himself to act upon it—to examine various and important neuralgic zones of our society which the North American experts let pass by unnoticed, either through ignorance or because these do not fall within their particular and personal spheres of interest.

We thus have the frequent spectacle of Puerto Rican specialists working exclusively in those avenues already traversed by the North American. This would not be objectionable if all the anthropological, sociological, historical, economic, and psychological areas of greatest importance had already been covered. This is not the case. And since in the few explored areas it is almost always the North American who enters first, one of two extreme reactions occurs: either the results of his initial labor are elevated to the level of dogma, unattackable and inexpugnable—Perloff's economic report occupied such a pedestal for many years—or an interminable series of articles appear, one after another, to corroborate, to contradict, or simply to comment on that initial research of the North American, as if there were not other virgin areas crying out for investigation by specialists, both native and foreign, employed by the Puerto Rican people.

The situation is aggravated by a fact suggested in these last words: the social scientist here is inevitably exposed to official directives. This is a tremendous misfortune, since state control comes to be the ideal psychological solution for the docile man, be he economist, educator, typist, or janitor.

Practically speaking, every center or agency where the social scientist works in Puerto Rico is, either directly or indirectly, funded by the government, and every one of them has its own official, dogmatic criteria inherited from North American experts. When one of our units announces some specific research or study one can, knowing the criteria of its directors, anticipate almost infallibly the "scientific" results of the study.

This sorry situation is the principal reason why the social sciences in Puerto Rico have not developed to the level of other fields and professions, do not fulfill their fundamental and inescapable mission, and do not have—with the exception of economics, whose mythical aureola of gold is furnished by the Industrial Development Company's millions—the respect and prestige which they should enjoy in Puerto Rican society.

A relatively high enrollment in the College of Social Sciences of the University of Puerto Rico does not contradict or detract from the statement. That the teaching profession is discredited in our environment does not prevent the much attacked School of Education from maintaining one of the highest enrollments recorded in our principal educational center. We all know, without need of research, that the immense majority of the Puerto Rican student body comes to the University today, not with the desire to learn or to create, but with a merely passive attitude. It is as if the University were an automatic machine which would furnish the student in a set period, preferably short, with the monthly check to subsidize forever the two classic financial entanglements of our modern world: the car and the FHA home.

With an attitude like that, it matters not at all to the "average" Puerto Rican student what college he enters, as long as the cost of his career is within the range of his pocketbook. The spectacle of this inert university mass, without an authentic vocation, ideals, orientation, or criteria of its own, cannot help but make us think, annoying as the coincidence may be, of that much-mentioned condition: docility.

Some specialist will try to sugar-coat this pill by assuring us that the same thing happens to North American students, for which reason we Puerto Ricans should not worry that ours are docile. We courteously refuse the expert's sugar-coating and reply that, if this is so, then we may chastise Puerto Rican and North American university students with complete impartiality. We are not one of those who cure or even find consolation for our own troubles in the troubles of others. And we see even less reason why the consolation must be greater because the "others" happen to be North Americans. The "scientific" tendency to ignore, cover up, excuse, harbor, or accept resignedly and impotently many of the problems which we suffer today, only because that problem was imported from North America, is an attitude which, barring error or omission, can only be attributed to the docile Puerto Rican. Faced with such "scientific" fatalism we believe that, if the social sciences in Puerto Rico are to serve only for ascertaining the North American genealogy of our problems and if these scientific disciplines are to lack the creative capacity to propose and defend original solutions of their own, we can, with complete tranquility and without any scruples, throw them overboard.

Having grasped this problem and foreseen the consequences, the historical thinker and humanist Justo Sierra, a man who was the opposite of provincial and chauvinistic, was already asking the Mexican students in 1910 at the inauguration of the National University of Mexico to plan "to acquire the means *to nationalize science, to 'Mexicanize' knowledge.*"

As long as Puerto Rico stays within a colonial-type economic and political structure, or to put it more justly, as long as Puerto Ricans prefer, consciously, to stay within such a structure, the development of all sciences, social and otherwise, will be precarious. The scientific spirit of the Puerto Rican is limited and conditioned by his attitude and his colonial mentality. Science cannot evolve freely here in order to put itself at the service of a Puerto Rican civilization, since such a concept (that of a Puerto Rican civilization) exists neither in reality nor—and this is the decisive point—in the will and the spirit of the Puerto Rican. Science is a universal and civilizing instrument, but in order to operate and develop fruitfully, it must do so today on a national plane. This at least is what the contemporary history of Germany, Russia, Japan, the United States, China, Israel, and others has proven. In Puerto Rico science functions provincially as a mere prop of the prevailing colonial system, with no appreciable creative capacity.

What the Puerto Rican has developed in the last two decades of material progress is not a true scientific spirit as some would have us think, but a new superstition:—that of believing that science is an *exclusive* product of the United States and that it can *only* be applied to and serve North American interests. This undoubtedly explains, among other things, the pathetic lack of results from the many years of scientific work in the University of Puerto Rico's Experimental Station. But let us not place the responsibility too heavily upon the individuals who have worked there. Their investigations had to be adapted, in their orientation and in their future practical application, to the colonial political and economic structure. Compare the achievements of science applied to agriculture in a country of scarce and poor land like Japan and the almost complete absence of achievement in this same area in Puerto Rico. Observe, as well, the miracle of applied science in the hands of an energetic, aggressive, and, above all, free nation like the Jewish one, as it converts the poor desert lands of contemporary Israel into productive agricultural zones. Listen, as a contrast, to the Puerto Rican's eternal lament of impotence with respect to the smallness of his island and the "irremediable" poverty of his soil. This attitude of impotence forces him to establish an artificial and anti-economic industrialization, completely independent of his agricultural realities and commercial necessities and dependent upon foreign interests, expediencies, and circumstances. Science is one and universal in Japan, Israel, and Puerto Rico. The difference lies both in the political freedom of Japan and Israel and in the nationalistic spirit—a spirit of national responsibility, if one prefers—of the Japanese and Israeli leaders and scientists, factors which are not present in Puerto Rico today.

The Psychological Function of the "Subversive" Writer: Easing the Pangs of Conscience

Since we have proposed to relate literary expression as far as possible to the psychological reality of the present-day Puerto Rican, it seems proper and opportune to point out a curious interrelation which has developed over the last twenty years between the dissident writer and the docile society in which he works.

We have seen how the social use of the euphemism has become accentuated (remember the semantic evolution of aplatanado-resigned-democratic), paralleling the increase in individual and collective docility. Yet, at the same time, the more docile and conformist Puerto Rican society has become, the more rebellious and aggressive the writer has become; the more extensive and intensive the social use of the euphemism, the more frank and open the literary expression; the more timid and cowardly the so-called *vox populi,* the more bold and firm the voice of its literature.

Naturally, these reactions are more common in writers of the latest generations. Detesting certain psychological and cultural traits which they judge to be negative and detrimental to the common good, they show unremitting enmity toward the euphemism. They cruelly and pitilessly crack open the sugar-coated pill and they "subversively" bludgeon the collective docility. With a probably accurate intuitive sense, they see the traditional Puerto Rican "virtues"—hospitality, courtesy, generosity—as gestures with which the docile man rationalizes his weakness. For this reason, undoubtedly, both the most representative writers and their work become daily less hospitable, courteous, and generous. Finding fault with the saying of the old Spanish hidalgo, this type of writer, because of his Puerto Rican experiences, seems to arrive at the conclusion that "courtesy *does* imply a lack of valor."[44] The conclusion is as valid (or as disputable) as any other, but it indicates the aggressively nonconformist attitude of the contemporary Puerto Rican writer.

One can be sure that this attitude encompasses general or universal traits. Every new generation is somewhat iconoclastic and reacts in a more or less violent manner against the world built by the previous generation, especially the one immediately previous, which appears in the eyes of the newcomers as the most responsible or, perhaps, the most "guilty." The intensity of the reaction depends upon the historical circumstances of the society in which the cyclical process is taking place. Every generation thus turns out to be, in its beginnings, nonconformist, rebellious, and at times, if the historical moment warrants it, openly revolutionary.

It is not, however, the general traits, but the specific or differentiating ones which interest us here. If we compare our writers with their contemporaries in the United States and England, we can begin to clarify what the Puerto Rican writers of the moment are and what they are not. The United States produced, as a phenomenon of the second postwar era, its Beat Generation, whose members are called beatniks, and England, its Angry Young Men.

The North American beatniks openly declare themselves defeated (it was one of their leaders who gave the movement its name) and hate the society of their country as it is constituted, but, lacking an ideology, they neither intend nor want to reform it. Their gesture of rebellion is, for all practical purposes, escapist: they separate themselves from society, living in smelly slums, immersed in alcohol and marihuana, and adopt an outward appearance of gutter bohemianism, expressed in argot, antisocial attitudes, gestures, and poses, so as to separate more pointedly the world of the squares from that of the beatniks. The North American Beat Generation cannot be frivolously dismissed, however, because of this disagreeable outward appearance. Their gesture is, after all, symbolic, and it must be accepted as an expression of their rebellion. The philosopher Diogenes also lived a dog's life in a shabby tub as a symbol of his scorn for the society of his time.[45]

There is nothing further removed from the North American beatniks than their contemporaries, the Angry Young Men of Great Britain. The young British writers know what they want: they detest their society but they do not flee from it. They wish to reform it and, therefore, they struggle against it, but from within. They come principally from the working class, but many become respected professors in colleges and universities until they become independent as writers and are able to live by their pens. And even though their works are devastating in their angry criticsm—because of which they may seem offensive to many Englishmen—they do not find it necessary to adopt a disreputable bohemianism to achieve their goal.

It is obvious that the Puerto Rican writers are closer to the angry young Englishmen than to the North American Beat Generation. Like those of England, the writers here know what they want. They make grave charges against Puerto Rican society, but they do not abandon it. They also want to reform their society. They struggle *against* it and *for* it, from *within* it. They are principally university graduates and almost all of them have government jobs. Although coming from diverse social strata, their standard of living is today, in general terms, that of the middle class. They do not practice nor are they interested in the greasy bohemianism of the beatniks, and they are even less interested in marihuana smoking. Neither do they try to elevate their individual faults or virtues to group norms. They are not antisocial in their external habits: they eat, drink, and dress like anyone else. Finally, they communicate with each other, not in a special language or private argot, but in the Spanish in use in Puerto Rico.

We should point out that this is not only true of the present generation; in general it has always been the attitude and the position of the writer in Puerto Rico. San Juan has never had its Montmartre nor its Greenwich Village. The writer in our society is not isolated in bohemian ghettos, whether assigned by society or chosen by the writers themselves, but is immersed in the social milieu. This is understandable in part because here the writer is not a professional, a man who lives by the pen, but a citizen with other obligations and responsibilities who writes in his free time. At first glance this could appear to be an advantage since, presumably, he would identify more with his society and be more concerned about it. Could this not be, however, a determining factor in explaining why the Puerto Rican writer has been often tolerant to an extreme of his society, too timid and considerate in his reproaches? Involved more than is suitable in the community to which he belongs, he perhaps fears or hesitates to antagonize it. Perhaps also this same immersion in the social group prevents him from acquiring sufficient objectivity to judge society as a whole. In one way or another, whether for these reasons or because of the general weakness for the euphemism and the circumlocution, many of our writers have tended to be excessively courteous, polite, and circumspect, sometimes to the point of ridiculousness. Isolated exceptions in diverse periods, such as Zeno

Gandía, Nemesio Canales, Lloréns Torres, Meléndez Muñoz, and Palés Matos, and to a lesser degree, Manuel Méndez Ballester, Emilio S. Belaval, and Salvador Tió, only serve to confirm the rule.

This tradition of literary circumspection was broken, perhaps more dramatically than on previous occasions, at the beginning of the forties when a still adolescent writer, José Luis González, in one of his first stories, placed in capital letters his first "swear word." From that moment on, Puerto Rican literature became "abusive" both in its vocabulary and in its intent. The writers of the youngest generations not only decided to call a spade a spade, but began to give a name to things which had never had them before in our literature. They brought into the literature themes and perspectives considered taboo in Puerto Rico. (It may be this latter fact which has led someone to describe this new Puerto Rican literature as demoniacal. It would be pertinent to ask, however, whether there is any esthetic expression which is not. Without the inner daemon, not even angelic writers would be able to create.)

There are, of course, correspondences between the course taken by Puerto Rican literature and that followed, with some years of difference, by other national Western literatures. However, what needs to be emphasized here is the psychological function of the new Puerto Rican literature (especially of that considerable portion which reflects social or political criticism) in relation to the society where it is produced. We are not referring to the social or ethical goals which the writer, as such, might have.[46] We are interested, rather, in showing how contemporary Puerto Rican society psychologically utilizes that aggressive literature with which its writers see fit to supply it, and which is, because of this very aggressiveness, so foreign and antagonistic to its collective docility.

It was not to be expected that a docile society would react aggressively to any literary challenge, but it might passively ignore it, letting it die of neglect. This is not the case here. The new literature which chastises and castigates society has been surprisingly successful, to the measure, of course, that success is possible for something Puerto Rican in present-day Puerto Rico. Is it desire for self-punishment? Not precisely. It seems to be a psychological escape valve, a sublimation of a collective guilt complex[47] through the frank and audacious comments of the writers. This will sound a bit like a spiritual purge or catharsis, but it is not, at least not in the classic sense. In the cathartic process the spectator purges himself spiritually through the literary work itself. Here the key to the situation is the fact that there are Puerto Ricans (the writers, in this case) capable of saying what society knowingly keeps secret. They make it possible for the social group, represented by the elite who are in contact with the literature, to ease its collective conscience. It is the same process which moves the Puerto Rican Rotarians to applaud with enthusiasm when a North American Rotarian points a critical finger at the linguistic politics of his organization: with his gesture the North American eases the conscience of the group. "Well, thank heavens"—the collective entity seems to reason— "at last someone says what it was my responsibility to say!" After which, the group, its conflict momentarily sublimated through the vicarious experience, again puts out of its mind the problem that began the conflict. There has been no purge or catharsis. The group is no better or worse than before the experience; it continues to be exactly the same:—docile and passive. But without those little "easings of the conscience," the Puerto Rican's deeply rooted colonial complexes would become insupportable.

It is paradoxical that society absorbs into its own peculiar colonial psychology an aggressive literature, ethical in intent, conceived to awaken consciences and to combat passivity and conformism, and makes it not only perfectly innocuous, but converts it into one more instrument of its psychological mechanism of docility. This explains why in contemporary Puerto Rican society the "subversive" writer is the object of tolerance and even of gratitude. After all, his writing is a totem of great value within the obscure mythology of collective docility.

"Easing the Pangs of Conscience" in the Field of Politics

This same phenomenon exists in the field of politics. One must observe the psychological role which the Independence Party has played in Puerto Rican society, particularly in relation to the majority party in power. It was impossible for the docile Puerto Rican society to assimilate within its psychological mechanism the nationalism of Albizu Campos. To make him innocuous the state had to destroy him physically. However, society easily absorbed the Independence Party, by a simple digestive process, since that political organism showed itself to be from the beginning a docilely Puerto Rican expression—its founders called it "democratic"—of the presumably revolutionary ideology it defended.

We have no interest, naturally, for the purposes of this analysis, in the faults of the Independence Party as such, but in its psychological function. The existence and survival, as part of the public life of the colony, of a pacific, tolerant, resigned, "democratic" independence party—an administrative party, in short, neither innovative nor revolutionary—is of vital importance within the general picture of Puerto Rican docility: it makes it easier for the collective guilt complex to be borne. Even the annexationists, perhaps without reasoning it through, would view with alarm the complete disappearance of this instrument. But it is the island governor, the leader of the majority party in power, who perceived the situation most clearly, perhaps because it posed a latent political problem within his own official family. He knows, in effect, that a substantial number of his followers of first and second rank are ex-Nationalists and former members of the Independence Party. Nothing can make him doubt the fidelity of these now unconditional followers, but the governor, a profound psychologist, had to provide them, just in case, with two psychological escape valves for their buried feelings.

The first consists of letting them cherish the faint hope that, in some remote moment in the future, if the providential circumstances justify it, he would "evolve" ideologically toward independence. Such a nebulous, confused, remote, and mystic hope for a very improbable "promised attitude"—equivalent to the psychological "promised land" of the Jewish leaders in the Old Testament—is something that, while seeming ingenuous and infantile to a rational mind, is always effective in the hands of an astute religious or political leader when dealing with a group of suggestible disciples. This fantasy is so deeply rooted in the minds of many ex-Nationalists and ex-independentistas in the Popular Party that not even the historic secret Cidra Meeting of 1960, when the governor revealed himself to them as more openly and brutally annexationist than the press and the people were permitted to perceive, served to unmask for them the chimera hidden behind a psychological trick as old as civilization itself.

The political leader—who in this case partly fulfills the function of mystical leader and, to a certain extent, of psychiatrist—provided the second way to "ease the pangs of conscience" by tolerating and even encouraging the legal existence of the Independence Party. It was the sacrificial lamb which, without being able to shoulder all the sins of the world, did, by nursing it vicariously and innocuously, assume the sin of favoring independence buried in the consciences of many Commonwealth supporters.[48]

What escape remains for the collective guilt complex with the recent disappearance of this opportune political tool? In order to understand the problem, we must examine to some extent the course of the Puerto Rican Independence Party and the surprising rise of the Christian Action Party.

The Independence Party died, at fourteen years of age, in the November 8, 1960, elections, not having achieved the minimum number of votes required by law. Of the 80,000 votes necessary for its survival — ten percent of the total electorate—it only obtained 24,000. Organized in the mid-forties, the Independence Party went to the polls for the first time in 1948. It achieved its greatest strength in the elections of 1952 with 125,000 votes, thus becoming, ephemerally, the second most important party in Puerto Rico. As soon as it had achieved this, its dramatic and vertiginous decline began. It will be the task of historians to analyze methodically and thoroughly the reasons for the decomposition and disappearance of this political entity from contemporary Puerto Rican life.

What we are interested in analyzing now is the reaction of the Puerto Rican people to what appeared then—months before the elections of 1960—as imminent: the disappearance of the Independence Party. In March of that year an idea took root and was speedily implemented, and months later, just a little before the elections, a new political group was registered: the Christian Action Party (P.A.C.).

The new organization appeared to have all the features it needed to attract to the ballot box an appreciable percentage of an electorate with escapist tendencies, enamoured of compromise. Cunningly, carrying its cynicism even further than the Popular Democratic Party had, the improvised P.A.C. totally evaded the fundamental moral problem: unachieved national sovereignty. It did not commit itself to independence, to annexation, or even to the present reformed colony. It promised instead, vaguely, the well-known "plebescite" for the future. As a compensation for such an immoral political attitude, it proclaimed itself the defender of Christian morality.

Among its founders and leaders there were an almost equal number of independentistas fleeing from the shipwrecked Independence Party as of Commonwealth adherents or annexationists discontented with their own party. Apparently, upon its registration, it counted among its potential electorate a considerable number of Popular Party members tired of continuism. In the political sphere, then, the P.A.C. came into being without any definite orientation or goals. Its social and economic aims were similarly ambiguous and disoriented. Among its proponents and advisors one finds fascist Spanish priests with the intransigent spirit of authentic inquisitors, imperialist and colonialist North American hierarchs and priests of a Catholicism with Protestant leanings, and Puerto Rican priests with conservative attitudes and Puerto Rican-ist tendencies. Their extreme reactionaryism with its core of cautious conservatism—an amalgam which permits only a limited diversity of like ingredients—prevented the formulation of an honest and sincere socioeconomic program of any significance and effectiveness. Does this mean that the P.A.C. was necessarily doomed to failure? Far from it. It would have had a good chance to survive in our environment except for one decisive error. Its very cowardice in the political, economic, and social realm, masked beneath the vaguely cohesive symbol of Catholicism, adequately fulfilled the docile Puerto Rican's psychological necessities.

Consciously or unconsciously, what its leadership attempted—and, as we know now, fully achieved—was to distract the electorate from the fundamental moral problem with which it was struggling as a people (its unresolved political status) at the moment when the death of the Independence Party appeared imminent. The unexpected religious issue injected into the electoral fight was one more smoke screen to hide the urgent political problem. They pretended to compensate for the defeat of political morality by posing the theme of religious morality. That kind of escapist instrument could not help but be attractive to the Puerto Rican. The P.A.C. could probably have had the support of many of the voters if the pastoral letters of the Catholic bishops had not appeared a few weeks before the elections.

The bishops, foreigners ignorant of the history, cultural patterns, and psychology of the people they were shepherding, wanted suddenly to channel Puerto Rican docility, which had always been a tributary of the state, toward the Church. This was an indescribable error in a country where four hundred years of colonial rule had dulled the people's sensitivity toward moral and religious values. For centuries faith and will had been yielded, by tradition, to the state. Suddenly faced with the alternative of channeling their docility toward the Church instead, the electorate to whom the demand was made would logically opt to be docile to the state. One cannot really even consider it an "option" but rather a routine continuation of a centuries-old tradition. As long as the P.A.C. maintained itself innocuously as a colonial administrative party, without political orientation or goals, it could have achieved some success. As soon as the bishops converted it into an alternative to traditional docility toward the state, they sealed their death sentence.

The ecclesiastical documents not only failed to hit their target (the party in power, which in this case embodied the state) but boomeranged against the Church, leaving brutally exposed its lack of spiritual ascendency over the colonial masses. Only foreign hierarchs, ignorant of Puerto Rican history and psychology, could have committed such a tremendous error.

The person who proclaims, either for a demagogic purpose or to ease his conscience, that the defeat of the Church at the ballot box is authentic proof of the Puerto Rican's lack of docility also makes a crass error. To turn one's back electorally on an institution in open decadence, which has no temporal power and only very precarious spiritual power in the society in which it operates, and to support openly the institution which is the depository of all the political, economic, and social power cannot honestly be qualified as an indocile, rebellious, or heroic act. Rather, it confirms the docile nature of the one who does it.

The Christian Action Party, in spite of its espousal of supposedly moral issues, failed to replace the moribund Independence Party—the only depository until then of the *one* moral issue in the colony—as the mitigator of the pangs of conscience of the Puerto Rican people. This was due not to the cynicism of its leadership, for cynicism is essential to any escapist political instrument, but rather to the political stupidity of the Catholic hierarchy.

The death of the Independence Party left society without an escape route for its obscure and buried anxieties within the accepted pattern of docility. The field is apparently free for the decisive struggle between the open and frank annexationism of the Statehood Party (in the opposition) and the masked annexationism of the Popular Party (in power). It seems probable, however, that no matter which of the two means is imposed to achieve the same hypothetical end, the collective entity will create, sooner or later, its own psychological instrument to ease the terrible guilt complex which afflicts it. How exactly Puerto Rican docility will contrive to do this before it is too late is something which no one today can predict.

One can see forming within official circles, however, the outlines of a new political strategem. This cannot, of course, be considered an authentic expression of the collective entity, but rather a structure imposed from above upon Puerto Rican docility to try to eliminate, once and for all, the vital political problem.

We refer to the establishment of a bipartisan system, copied from the North American tradition, through which the only two parties operating on the island—both in favor of assimilation or annexation—would become docile branches of the respective parties in the United States: Democratic and Republican. In this way, officially at least, independence would be declared dead.

To make the maneuver effective, the island legislature, at the request of the governor, has approved a rejuvenated electoral law which makes practically impossible the registration of a new party in Puerto Rico unless, of course, it is registered with official sponsorship, utilizing the powerful machinery of the party in power. Although the apparent motive has been to prevent the Christian Action Party from registering again, and the "democratic" excuse was to make the electoral law stricter to prevent possible fraud, the real purpose is to destroy any possibility of opposition, from the ballot box, to the political idea upheld by the only two parties in existence: annexation. At this moment in Puerto Rico, practically speaking, only one party operates, since the Popular Democratic Party in power and the Statehood Republican Party in the opposition differ little in political terms, and could be merged, without much trouble, in one group which it would be fitting to call the *Sole Party for Permanent Union with the United States.* Even the most enthusiastic cultivators of political escapism would have to admit that the recent maneuver leaves so-called "Puerto Rican democracy" very much open to doubt.

If the strategem should evoke criticism in Latin America, the possibility always remains that the Governor, in a move of pure democratic hypocrisy, could order the creation behind the scenes of a new party, mobilizing for this purpose all the governmental machinery (the only way, we now know, in which it is at present feasible to register a political group in Puerto Rico). This puppet party could even display gracefully in its platform the ideal of independence. Such a possibility seems, however, somewhat remote. The Popular Democratic Party, decrepit, stiff-jointed, and cynical, no longer feels the insistent need to keep up appearances as it did in earlier years. Today the democratic farce is much less important to it than the obsessive fear of organized opposition.

In either case, the official game, from 1898 on, has always been the same. Today as yesterday, it can best be described by that painful yet immortal epithet: "burundanga."[49]

Conclusion

In summary, we do not think that we have proved anything "objectively," an exercise which we do not practice, and which does not interest us because, among other reasons, we wish to remain faithful to our scientific spirit. But we have pointed the way toward a rational analysis of the personality of the contemporary Puerto Rican from the perspective of his docility. We have also shown how our literature dramatizes many facets of that personality. This attempt at analysis cannot be considered exhaustive. Several significant elements—Puerto Rican music, a true expression of our docility as a people, for instance—we left untouched, not so much to save space as not to destroy too much the unity announced in our subtitle.

Nor have we taken the trouble to examine Puerto Rico's submissive acceptance of actions of the military, such as the occupation and despoilment of Vieques by the United States Navy (the tragic aspects of which have been expressed by Pedro Juan Soto in his novel *Usmaíl*) or the installation on the docile island soil, without any consultation or agreement, of two powerful atomic bases, primary targets in the event of a Russian-American war, which all the states along the Atlantic coast sensibly and energetically rejected. The reason is clear: that which was brutally and obviously colonial did not interest us in this analysis of the Puerto Rican personality.

A recent circumstance, which it would be premature, perhaps, to submit to rigorous analysis, but which should be closely watched because of its serious political, social, and moral consequences, is the surprising incrustation of thousands of Cuban exiles on Puerto Rican society. This is not the first time in the island's history when American struggles for liberty tossed their political residues upon our shores. At the victorious conclusion of the fight for independence in South America, South American emigrants, primarily from Venezuela, found a comfortable refuge in the Puerto Rican colony. They were, naturally, unconditional supporters of Spain, sworn enemies of independence for our America, and systematic haters of liberty. There is no doubt that nineteenth-century Puerto Rican colonialist conservatism and conformism received a decisive reinforcement from these reactionary families who stubbornly turned their backs upon the future of Spanish America.

History repeats itself today with the Cuban exiles. Unconditional supporters of the United States and cynically colonialist, they ally themselves on their arrival with the most obviously retrograde and anti–Puerto Rican forces in the colonial society. Protected by the Federal Government, by the native officialdom, and by annexationist circles, they become, automatically, bitter enemies of Puerto Rican national sovereignty and dignity. Save for a few always honorable exceptions, they are in the best of cases aggressive and unscrupulous in their struggle for survival, rapidly displacing from their jobs the docile Puerto Ricans, who have no laws of their own to protect them from such unexpected competition. And, besides, the timid natives have discovered, all too soon, that to protest against the disloyal competition or the strident arrogance of the recent arrivals is to expose oneself to being called a "Communist" and to attract to oneself all the political, social, and economic sanctions which such a term carries with it in North

American territory, no matter how false it may be. Docilely, once again, the Puerto Ricans endure and keep silent, playing with exemplary meekness their traditional role as a "generous," "hospitable," and "democratic" people.

In spite of the fact that the number of Cuban exiles may seem slight in relation to the total population of the island, one should not underestimate their influence, since in the short period of two years these admirably protected newcomers have infiltrated, especially in the metropolitan area, every institution—from the Church to the brothel— many of them occupying key positions in governmental agencies, the University, professional circles, civic organizations, industry, banking, commerce, and crime. Even more serious is the fact that they have taken control of radio and television stations and have infiltrated the daily press, from which they proclaim, with official applause, their cynical message of submission to the already very submissive Puerto Ricans. This is an unexpected twentieth-century reinforcement to native docility and conformism. Its moral, political, and social consequences are not difficult to predict and should be studied at the right moment.

We also would find revealing a methodical but not exhaustive psycho-linguistic study of Puerto Rican popular speech in the light of the docility theory: intonation, phonetics, syntax, semantic values, the use of the euphemism and the circumlocution, the most common images, sayings, etc. For it, one could take as a point of departure the excellent study done here by Tomás Navarro Tomás.[50]

In spite of these and other possible gaps we think we have shown throughout the analysis that there is scarcely an area in Puerto Rican society where, scratching the surface a little, docility does not appear as a constant and determining trait.

Appendix[51]

An important factor which we suppose has been inferred, given the centuries-long colonial condition of Puerto Rico, but which we have not studied in detail has been and is, under both Spanish and North American regimes, the *disproportionate* number of forces of official repression of the civil population *in relation to* the small geographic size of the island.

Within our present society—a colony of aerodynamic design—which guarantees the right to the enjoyment of several civil liberties, the complicated network of official repression which constantly threatens precisely those same liberties is not immediately obvious.

Although the methods of repression today are naturally much more skillful and subtle than they were a century ago, this fact is irrefutable.

One could allege, on the one hand, that what we are calling repressive forces operate in almost all contemporary states and, on the other, that we are calling "repressive forces" some which commonly operate in other countries as mere public service agencies. Certainly. But in the first case what we are trying to point out is the disproportion and duplication of the repressive forces not only in relation to the geographic area of the island, but also to the traditionally peaceful state of our country. In the second case, some public service agencies which we will point out as repressive in Puerto Rico emanate, in free and sovereign countries, from the will and authority of the people themselves while, in our country, these (federal) agencies are imposed on us by the imperial regime and controlled by it. There is, then, a virtual, practical, and legal difference between the two cases, as will be seen below.

Today (December 1965) the two most notoriously repressive federal agencies operate on the island: the C.I.A. (the North American Intelligence Service, the official agency of international espionage and terrorism, with an astronomical budget and complete freedom of action, which uses sabotage, bribery, blackmail, assassination, and the like in every country of the modern world)[52] and the F.B.I. (the Federal Bureau of Investigation, which does not operate with the brutally terroristic methods of the C.I.A.).[53] We have, as well, the Intelligence Service of the United States Army,[54] the Federal Immigration Service,[55] the Federal Postal and Customs Services,[56] and the Federal Communications Commission.[57]

The local government has contributed modestly on its part to the repression of its people. Besides the logical police force to maintain public order, it maintains:

1. The detective branch (of the Puerto Rican police).
2. The Shock Troop (a special body within the police).
3. An Internal Security Service.[58]
4. A recently created Puerto Rican F.B.I. (One infers from this that the federal one is not sufficiently effective in Puerto Rico.)
5. The National Guard, maintained with combined funds, both federal and island. (This repressive military body is not to be confused with the North American army on the island.)

One must add to these a considerable number of Cuban exiles who, on their own initiative in many cases (perhaps subsidized by Washington in others), have constituted themselves as a civil body of espionage, denunciation, and pressure (almost equivalent to repression) against the Puerto Ricans.[59] And, finally, several private detective agencies exist which upon occasion cooperate or collaborate with the official repressive forces.

We must reckon, nevertheless, with something more decisive: a latent and constant threat, a tremendous sword of Damocles always suspended, not only above the Puerto Rican population but above the whole Caribbean area in particular and Latin America in general. Puerto Rico held, until November 30, 1965, the doubtful privilege of housing upon its docile soil nine military and naval bases and stations, atomic and non-atomic. This was the greatest concentration of North American military bases and stations anywhere on earth, including any point of equal geographic area within the United States itself. Although the Puerto Rican does not reason it out, nor does the fact operate on the conscious level, it has undoubtedly been instrumental in adding greater collective submissiveness to the docility of our people during the last thirty years.

On December 8, 1965, following the general policy of reducing and dismantling now useless military bases, in the United States as well as in those nations and territories where the North Americans maintain military forces, the Secretary of Defense in Washington announced that the federal government would return to the island government about 15,000 cuerdas[60] of land corresponding to small army bases and totally obsolete military posts, including the historic San Felipe del Morro Castle (rebaptized by the North Americans as Fort Brook). Naturally, all Puerto Ricans must be pleased at repossessing these small pieces of land on an island where land is scarce and valuable. But we must not forget that there remain in federal hands, for military purposes, hundreds of thousands of cuerdas of the best and most productive Puerto Rican coastal terrain, and that the obsolete military posts abandoned today signify nothing if we compare them with the powerful naval base at Vieques, that of Culebras, the enormous air base of Ramey Field in Aguadilla, and the one with the remote-controlled atomic rockets and the submarines (the most menacing in the whole Caribbean area) at Ceiba, as well as the lesser military posts on the island.[61]

Since we are dealing with a small island in universal geography (a smallness which the regime has made us swallow ad nauseam until it has become a collective complex), inhabited by a traditionally peaceful population, the phenomenon of such a complex duplication of repressive forces is little less than inexplicable. We Puerto Ricans should, after all, be proud of the absolute terror that our docility has unleashed, in Washington as much as in San Juan, especially during the last thirty years. (Might the leaders in both capitals have heard and believed that adage: "May God free me from calm waters, for from the rough water I shall free myself?") Apparently, this colonial nation, with no arms of its own and no liberating army, made docile to the saturation point by "the system," has a greater capacity and power to make the so esteemed, loved, admired, and venerated North American empire blow up with a tremendous universal explosion than the immense and mighty atomic powers such as Soviet Russia and Communist China. At any rate, given the disproportionate quantity of official repressive forces, it is obvious that they are afraid of us as a people. That is to say, in spite of our docility, we are feared not only by the local government which presumably represents us, but by the richest and most devastatingly powerful empire of the contemporary Western world, of which we are a colony. This, necessarily, should make all Puerto Ricans feel big and important, no matter what their political ideology. Or should it?

Appendix 2. The Pro-Independence Movement in Puerto Rico: The Need for Analysis

It now seems opportune to attempt to analyze, from the perspective of the psychological problem of docility, the militant and controversial Pro-Independence Movement. It holds the credit for having revived, with its founding eight years ago, the ideal of independence at the moment when it seemed almost moribund and for having, thereafter, sustained it forcefully in public debate.

An offshoot of the Puerto Rican Independence Party around 1958, the M.P.I. was originally conceived as a mass movement, to become later a politically sophisticated or politicized elite—extremist and "comecandela"[62]—but cut off, in spite of it all, from the Puerto Rican masses.

It is impossible, of course, to make a psychological analysis of this organization within the space limitations of this brief appendix. One could guess, however, that its fiery and anarchic extremism or "comecandelismo," which often seems to trace an unconscious suicidal trajectory in the particular political environment of Puerto Rico, as well as its excessive admiration for, identification with, and imitation of foreign models perhaps reveal the same traits of Puerto Rican docility already found in other local political groups.

The Puerto Rican Short Story of the Forties Generation

To José Luis González, pioneer of the 1940 generation of short story writers.

To Dr. Concha Meléndez, the first student of our literature who gave importance to the short story writing of that generation.

It is merely a lack of intelligence to refuse the experience embodied in the past; but it shows an even greater lack of intelligence to refuse the experience embodied in the present.

Herbert Read, *The Nature of Literature*

Antecedents: The Thirties Generation

The so-called thirties generation, which preceded the short story writers whose work concerns us here, appears to us today as a definitive and significant phenomenon in the history of our literature. It is, perhaps, the first group which was aware of the existence of a national will.

That generation's orientation was nourished by the hidden talents of isolated figures from our literary past. It seems probable that it took from Manuel Zeno Gandía the implacable objectivity with which he viewed the surrounding world, a dramatic and effective literary technique; from Miguel Meléndez Muñoz his profound sociological concerns; from Luis Lloréns Torres his eagerness to poeticize indigenous characteristics, an interest which had a noble and remote precedent in Manuel Alonso's *El Gíbaro*. Nemesio Canales' ironic point of view also must have influenced one or another of the writers of that generation who have successfully delved into irony. Emilio S. Belaval with his *Cuentos Para Fomentar el Turismo* immediately

Author's note: This essay is the prologue to *Cuentos Puertorriqueños de Hoy* (3rd ed., selection, prologue, and notes by René Marqués; Rio Piedras: Editorial Cultural, 1971).

74

comes to mind. This ironic vein is not, however, characteristic of the bulk of this literature. Realism, "costumbrismo," social consciousness, and poetic revaluation of the characteristically Puerto Rican are the notes which blend to different degrees in the writing of these fruitful years.

The most significant aspect of the decade is the writers' conscious effort to achieve an authentically Puerto Rican position in the face of two serious problems: the island writers' traditional literary dependence on Spain, and the alarming North American political, economic, and cultural penetration.

The problem transcended the literary field, and its posing was a matter of national urgency. *Revaluation* seems to be the key word of those years. In the political arena, nationalist sentiment became more acute, and the need for immediate social reform became obvious. In literature, Hispanic studies proliferated and serious and responsible investigations of Puerto Rican culture were begun. Antonio S. Pedreira and Tomás Blanco, among others, explored in their essays problems crucial to our personality and our destiny as a people.

The results were visible in a lessening of "colonial" dependence on peninsular Spanish literature, and in a greater awareness of national values, which would then form a barricade against North American political and cultural penetration. The Puerto Rican writer thus recognized his Spanish roots, but he now felt more able to make his own contribution to the linguistic world to which he belonged.

In addition, the narrative genres began to explore a new world already discovered by the poets: Spanish America. Concha Meléndez' pioneering Spanish American studies were a valuable guide for the creative writers. The Spanish American novel "of the land" had a more decisive influence than the Spanish novel on the Puerto Rican narrative writers in the thirties. Enrique A. Laguerre is the best—if not the only—exponent of the new insular novel which came out of the literary movement of that decade.

Drama, like fiction in many ways, was jolted by a current of change. The small group of dramatic and comic playwrights of the thirties generation swept our stages clean of neoclassicism and romanticism, tiresome relics of the past century which were still permitted to appear on local stages.

In some ways, at least, the theater went beyond the narrative genres. One could mention, for example, its overcoming of "costumbrismo," which never disappeared completely from the short story production of that period. In general terms, poetry, theater, and the essay covered more ground in those years than the short story and the novel. Except for isolated cases among the narrative writers, such as Laguerre and Belaval, we do not find a group conscious of a regenerative mission. On the contrary, along with the social realism and the "costumbrismo" of the decade, the already out-of-date modernist form (and even the romantic mode) of the short story were still widely cultivated.

The Forties Generation

The generation of young narrators who reached their literary maturity, or started writing in the decade of the forties, began their task very much as a logical continuation of the thirties movement which preceded them. The young writers benefited, moreover, from the ties broken by their predecessors: they did not feel inferior to contemporary peninsular literature. One might also add the important historic fact that Spanish literature, during the years from the civil war (1936) to the end of the Second World War (1946), seemed to be, in the narrative genres, and viewed from Puerto Rico, little less than a desert. Perhaps this is because the military conflicts had closed practically every means of literary communication between the two contemporary worlds: the Spanish and the Puerto Rican. After the generation of 98, Spain seemed to offer us very little.

The young writers turned toward Spanish America, but two circumstances served to limit that horizon. The Second World War had also obstructed the slight communication with these countries. And the precedent established by the Puerto Rican narrators of the thirties had not been sufficiently far reaching to create an awareness of the vanguard of novelistic and short story expression in Spanish America, although it was precisely with this movement that our writers would have had the greatest affinity. Not even the Argentine Eduardo Mallea, already well known in those years, was discovered or studied, nor his work disseminated by the Puerto Rican writers of the thirties.

The most alert spirits in the new generation began to feel disappointed. They wanted to go beyond Quiroga, beyond indigenism, beyond the "novel of the land" of the Gallegos type, beyond, also, Juan Bosch's type of social realism. They turned then toward an available and virgin field: contemporary North American literature. They explored it thoroughly and it led them, by a logical detour, to the new English and European literature, the latter read in English translations published in the United States.

The always precarious communication with Latin America in the publishing field was completely stabilized after the Korean War, and by then, in the mid-fifties, the young Puerto Ricans, at the height of their production, began to discover that others had been doing what they were now doing in Puerto Rico: among them, the Argentine Jorge Luis Borges, the Cuban Lino Novás Calvo and, still later, the Venezuelan Guillermo Meneses in his last period. There is a notable affinity between this handful of Spanish Americans and various Puerto Rican writers of the forties generation. Though belonging to different age groups they had found inspiration in identical foreign literary sources and were children, moreover, of the same epoch with similar esthetic sensibilities and preoccupations. It goes without saying that the Spanish Americans enjoyed obvious advantages by comparison to the young Puerto Rican writers: in the first place, the maturity and refinement they had achieved through an already considerable literary apprenticeship; in the second place, a command of their own language, an always critical problem for the "bilingual" Puerto Rican writer. The Puerto Ricans of the new generation have, though, an advantage as well: their very youth, conscious and alert, which can perhaps carry them further, if they persevere, than the already expert Spanish American writers have gone.

In at least one way, the new generation faithfully followed the trajectory indicated by the island writers of the thirties. Like their predecessors, they engaged in an implacable, exhaustive exploration of their native roots, so as then to transpose this material to the poetic plane. However, the writers also contributed something of their own to the national literature. And it is this contribution which to a great extent determines the tone of the literature during the eleven-year period 1948–59.

Like the previous generation, that of the forties discovers new sources of drama in immediate reality and thus incorporates fresh themes into Puerto Rican literature. It also introduces, for the first time in our contemporary literature, serious metaphysical concerns. The existential problem of man is the central theme of a good part of the new writing, either replacing or becoming integrated with the social and political concerns of the Puerto Rican. They perhaps achieve here what was tried with only partial success in the thirties: a literary focus which combines deep autochthonous roots with a broad universal appeal.

Another obvious contribution of the young writers is their formal and stylistic innovations inspired by esthetic-literary trends in France, England, and the United States. Our narrative and dramatic genres can thus be accepted without hesitation as part of contemporary Western literature. The present is perhaps one of the few moments in the history of Puerto Rican literature when its prose style has been in step with the esthetics prevailing in the West.

One must understand, however, that, although the innovations came mainly from the new generation, various of the writers of the thirties generation who are still literarily active have moved toward the same new currents. A good example of this is the Enrique A. Laguerre of *La Ceiba en el Tiesto*. Similarly, when the thirties movement began, some writers belonging to the twenties generation joined the innovative currents of that decade: a natural and logical process in the development of every national literature.

Characteristics of the New Literature

Themes

Under the decisive influence of their own historical background— Puerto Rico from 1940 to 1959—these writers incorporate new themes into our literature. The Puerto Rican Nationalist phenomenon, industrialization and its moral, psychological, and social consequences, Puerto Rican participation in the Korean War, time as a philosophic problem, and the existential solitude of man, are representative themes. Simultaneously, the writer moves away from rural life to plunge into the problems of the city dweller. It is José Luis González with his collection of stories *El Hombre en la Calle* who takes this new path in 1948.

But there is another significant fact: the appearance of women as protagonists in the new literature. The dramatists and the narrative writters of the forties generation seem able to create feminine characterizations of tragic intensity and psychological depth. Until then the female character had been no more than a secondary figure in our literature. Even on the few occasions where she appeared as the heroine of the story, she did not completely achieve her emancipation as a vigorous and independent creation. The story could revolve around her, but she was not, in the last analysis, responsible for the unleashing of the dramatic action. Perhaps following models long established in our society, the woman in Puerto Rican literature was not able to achieve, as a character, the right to be a conscious creator of circumstances.

The Puerto Rican feminist movement had already obtained political equality, but it had not been able—nor had it actually asked or attempted—to destroy the established social and cultural structure. It was in the forties that Puerto Rican society made a rapid turn toward the Anglo-Saxon—style matriarchy. The cultural and ethical patterns of a social structure based on the tradition of the paterfamilias rapidly deteriorated. They succumbed with such dizzying speed that it became clear that these patterns and values were held in little esteem by Puerto Rican society.

This may explain why the female frequently has a prominent role in the literature today. Perhaps it also explains why she does not always appear in a flattering light. Those responsible for that literature have lived through the initial vogue of the North American matriarchal model in Puerto Rico and have not been able to accept with the docility of their opposite numbers in the United States the role of mere providers.

Landscape

It is revealing to discover the new perspective the young authors bring to bear on their own landscape. They do not see their country any more as an "Island of Enchantment" or a "Pearl of the Seas." The landscape which enraptured our romantic poets and which our "costumbrista" writers lovingly highlighted comes to occupy a very secondary place in the bulk of our fictional writing. Man and his problems—political, social, psychological, or metaphysical—overshadowed any vision of the landscape and, on occasion, eclipsed it completely.

When the short story writer of the forties generation gives an important role to landscape, he almost always uses it as it relates to the psychology of the protagonist. The natural background, described or perceived fragmentarily through the landscape, reveals his state of mind. The landscape, in other words, becomes subjective. In the hands of the writer it is now a "functional" instrument, not a description for esthetic pleasure per se.

Moreover, since the place of the action has been transferred from the country to the city, the background scenery is primarily urban. Streets, factories, apartment buildings, lampposts, telephone wires, neon lights, advertisements, airports, stores, towers of steel, shantytown houses, tourist hotels, brothels, restaurants, buses, bars, in short everything that appears daily before the eyes of the city dweller, make up the landscape of a good part of the literary output of this period.

Focus

With the abandonment of the rural zone, the writer generally also abandons the "costumbrista" focus. In the short story, the most representative writers of the new generation no longer cultivate that pleasant and picturesque mode much appreciated in the previous periods: the vignette or sketch.

also has complete control of the language. But it can degenerate into unintentional confusion or into pure nonsense in the unsure hands of a neophyte. Joyce in English and Faulkner in North American literature have used it with mastery.

As to technical devices, the most important one to be incorporated into contemporary Puerto Rican literature is stream of consciousness or the interior monologue. Of French origin, this device has its probable roots in the psychoanalytic theories of Sigmund Freud. It was in Anglo-Saxon literature, however, that it was subsequently developed until it reached esthetic perfection in the Englishwoman Virginia Woolf, the Irishman James Joyce, and, among the North Americans, in the Southerner William Faulkner.

It becomes a little difficult to separate this technical device from the second stylistic mode which we described above, perhaps because the interior monologue is often expressed through that style. Stream of consciousness attempts to give us the subconscious thought processes of the character in all its complex tangle of images, associations, and reactions. We said, in speaking of style, that it is a question of giving the *sensation* of whirlwind or chaos: nothing more. From the authentic chaos of the world which lies beyond consciousness, the writer has to extract an esthetically coherent and logical world. But, and this is perhaps the truly difficult part, it must not be so coherent and logical that we lose the *sensation* of a disjointed world which is judged to be an attribute of the subconscious. If we were able to discern the work and effort expended by the author to achieve this exact and dangerous equilibrium, the device would lose its effectiveness. The task is nothing more nor less than the utilization of an almost scientific rigor to create, literarily, a psychological process which gives us the sensation of something incoherent and chaotic, *without being so.* For the purposes of the work of art—story or novel—each image, each association, each *apparent* incoherence of the process must fulfill a function, have a motive, and be rigorously logical with respect to the psychological, dramatic, and esthetic *whole* of the narration.

This device has various modes. It will be sufficient, I think, to mention two of them. The first, the direct one, consists of literally capturing a mental or interior monologue of the character. In order to differentiate this silent flow of images and associations from the rest of the narration, it is usual to present it typographically in italics. In more complicated forms in which there actually exist monologues within monologues, other typographical devices are used as well: boldface or quotation marks, for example. At times, the story or novel is almost entirely an interior monologue, since the narration is told through the chaotic stream of consciousness of one or more individuals. This latter is the case in *As I Lay Dying,* one of William Faulkner's most successful works. Then, if the author prefers, the typographic convention of the italics is unnecessary.

The second mode, the indirect one, consists of making the exterior world subjective by filtering it through the character's mind, but without having recourse to the formal structure of the monologue. Landscape, objects, human beings, external actions all have, thanks to the skillful recounting of the author, special repercussions in the character; they create associations and reactions which are not those which we would objectively judge as adequate to the circumstances. That is to say, the world described by the narrator is not the objective world as it exists, but rather as it is obscurely perceived by the mind of a specific character. Thus, we get results identical to those produced by the previous technique, since we also penetrate into the stream of consciousness of the individual, perceiving *indirectly,* in this case, his "interior monologue." The two techniques are frequently fused in one literary work.

Another technical device frequently used today, in narrative literature as well as in the theater and the movies, is montage or insertion of retrospective scenes. This consists of dramatizing, within a specific moment of the present action, scenes from the past as *live material.* This technique is often fused in fiction with that of interior monologue.

The Authors

Eight authors—Abelardo Díaz Alfaro, José Luis González, René Marqués, Pedro Juan Soto, Edwin Figueroa, José Luis Vivas, Emilio Díaz Valcárcel, and Salvador de Jesús—are representative, we think, of the new literature. Some of them have been the real innovators of the contemporary short story in Puerto Rico, and with them the genre achieves a degree of technical and esthetic perfection which has seldom been reached in our literature. Prior to this, only Emilio S. Belaval, with his excellent *Cuentos Para Fomentar el Turismo,* had been able to take the Puerto Rican short story out of its traditional molds, opening the way for more radical innovation.

These young authors, the oldest not yet forty, the youngest around thirty, constitute, for the most part, a nucleus of professional writers.[3] This is true, not in the sense that they can live from their writing, something impossible in our environment, but in that they possess a profound knowledge of their craft, a high degree of professional responsibility, an almost missionary dedication to the creative task, and an urgent, vital desire to excel personally and collectively. That is, almost all of them are conscious of themselves not only as individual creators, but as members of a generation, of a group similar in sensibility, esthetic ideals, social and political perception, and historical placement.

With the exception of José Luis González, an active Marxist for a good number of years, the short story writers represented here keep themselves more or less on the margin of party struggles. They are not obviously committed to any island faction. The majority put forth their ideals with aggressive independence, without yielding to the rigid discipline of a party. The minority feels allergic to, or perhaps disgusted at, the mere mention of the word "politics."[4] This is not, however, the result of a group stand, but rather the consequence of a personal and spontaneous intellectual attitude toward the independent mission of the creative artist in the society to which he belongs.

Other Cultivators of the Genre

Although we deem these authors to be the most representative short story writers in Puerto Rico today, others of the forties generation have written in that genre, among them the poets Juan Martínez Capó and Violeta López Suria, the latter bringing her personal lyrical touch to brief psychological sketches. José Emilio (or Josemilio, as he often prefers to sign himself) González, initially a poet but principally an exuberant, rhetorical, and indefatigable literary reviewer, has also written some surrealistic short stories.

Julio Marrero Núñez, author of historical dramas, has written, logically, historical stories. In *Requiem por un Soldado del Rey de España*, his best up till now, he skillfully adapts to the new style.

Esther Feliciano Mendoza, an assiduous cultivator of the "costumbrista" vignette, has made a valuable contribution to the little-cultivated mode of the children's short story. The author's sentimental and lyric expression nourishes themes and a style of folkloric and native flavor.

Authors of the same generation who have also cultivated the genre are Arturo Parrilla, Héctor Barrera, Juan Enrique Colberg Petrovich, Gerard Marín, Ferdinand Jiménez Arroyo (whose short stories have been published in *Alma Latina* under the pen name of J. Jiménez A.), and María Teresa Serrano de Ayala. Manuel del Toro, Silás Ortiz Valentín, the little-known author of humorous stories about peasants, and Luis Quero Chiesa can be mentioned because, although earlier in chronological age, they either began writing during the last fifteen years, or were incorporated into the literary production of this period. The last, along with Marrero Núñez, writes historical short stories: his *José Campeche* won the second prize in the 1955 Short Story Contest of the Ateneo Puertorriqueño.

As is natural in every literary period, coexisting with the new literature are writers who, because of their esthetic perspective, expression, and criteria, belong to previous generations. Of this group, the fiction writers closest or most similar to the forties generation seem to be Enrique A. Laguerre, Emilio S. Belaval, and Tomás Blanco. Less close, we think, because of the traditional focus they give to the short story or because of their cultivation of the legend, or the literary sketch, are, among others, Miguel Meléndez Muñoz, José S. Alegría, and Vicente Palés Matos.

Also a natural part of the historical cycle is the appearance in this decade of a small group of younger writers who constitute what in the future will have to be called the "generation of the fifties." They are now in their formative years, and their first literary attempts do not yet furnish a sufficiently solid base upon which to give a judgment or to risk a prophecy. Time will tell whether it is these or others still unknown who will take from the hands of the forties generation the responsibility for further developing the modern Puerto Rican short story.[5]

Possible Causes of the Present Boom

We have discovered various possible causes for the short story boom in Puerto Rico during the last ten or twelve years. In the first place, we have the fortunate appearance of a pioneer nucleus of young writers, led by José Luis González. Later stimuli would perhaps not have had such rapid and effective results without the resolute labor of this small nucleus. And furthermore, we believe that the stimuli which the short story received in literary circles and in the Ateneo from 1953 on were in great part motivated by the existence of a base which justified them: the work of the original group.

The literary contests of various university groups and the appearance of the Saturday literary page of *El Mundo,* which made room, in its limited space, for the works of both well-known writers and beginning authors were a stimulus, on a more modest level, for the neophyte or amateur.

On the professional level, and contributing effectively to the development, maturity, and purification of the genre, there have been the annual literary contests of the Ateneo Puertorriqueño, which, since 1953, has sponsored the Christmas Festival, and the work of the magazine

Asomante, whose rigorous criteria of selection have rarely permitted narrations of doubtful esthetic quality to slip into its pages.

The short story writers of the forties generation have, as well, to give special recognition to Dr. Concha Meléndez. She was the first student and investigator of Puerto Rican literature to give full importance to the work of the young fiction writers. Through prologues, articles, and essays, and in her work as anthologist, she studied and disseminated the new styles and modes of the Puerto Rican short story.

In spite of the natural lacunae which pioneer works of this type may contain, the appearance of two fundamental works, the first *Diccionario de Literatura Puertorriqueña* by Dr. Josefina Rivera de Álvarez (1955) and the first *Historia de la Literatura Puertorriqueña* by Dr. Francisco Manrique Cabrera (1956), was a valuable stimulus and encouragement, not only to the short story, but to all our literature. Of equal importance is the inclusion of Puerto Rican narrators of the forties generation in the second edition of the Argentine Enrique Anderson Imbert's *Historia de la Literatura Hispanoamericana,* published by the Fondo de Cultura Económica in Mexico in 1957.

The Department of Education's use of Abelardo Díaz Alfaro's *Terrazo* as a textbook has awakened interest in the school-age adolescent. On the university level, both the Department of Hispanic Studies and the Department of General Studies of the University of Puerto Rico are beginning to pay attention to the contemporary Puerto Rican short story. This is due not so much to official university policy but to the initiative of some professors who have felt a responsibility for acquainting their students with our most recent literature.

Various anthologies of Puerto Rican short stories have appeared in recent years. In 1954, Enrique A. Laguerre prepared, for pedagogical purposes, a collection of legends, sketches, and short stories for the Department of Public Education. The magazine *Asomante* published an anthology issue on the Puerto Rican short story in 1956. Concha Meléndez did a collection for the Puerto Rican government in 1957 and another for a New York editor in 1959. Before that (1956) Professor Paul J. Cooke, of Monticello College, had published in the United States an *Antología de Cuentos Puertorriqueños.*

Of greater importance, perhaps because it is proof of the crossing of frontiers, is the inclusion of young Puerto Rican authors in foreign anthologies of Spanish and Spanish American short stories. Robert E. Osborne, in his *Cuentos del Mundo Hispanico* (1957), included one by Abelardo Díaz Alfaro. The Chilean critic Ricardo Latcham selected a story by René Marqués for his *Antología del Cuento Hispanoamericano*

(1958). In an anthology issue on Spanish American literature translated into English, the magazine *New World Writing* (1958) published the English version of a short story by José Luis González.

Works by various authors of this generation have appeared in foreign magazines: in Europe and the United States, translations into Czech, Swedish, Russian, and English of stories by José Luis González, René Marqués, and Abelardo Díaz Alfaro; in Spanish America and Spain, stories by José Luis González, René Marqués, Pedro Juan Soto, and Emilio Díaz Valcárcel.

Professors of departments of Romance languages of various North American universities have done studies either of the new Puerto Rican short story in general or of individual works, publishing articles and reviews in *Books Abroad* and other literary magazines in English, and in university publications like Columbia's *Revista Hispánica*.

Finally, the recognition which has been given to the new Puerto Rican short story in responsible critical circles and in the serious press of the Spanish-speaking world is an encouragement to the young writers. The short story collections of José Luis González, Abelardo Díaz Alfaro, René Marqués, Pedro Juan Soto, and Emilio Díaz Valcárcel have been received as valuable contributions to the short story genre in the Spanish language in Spain as well as in Mexico, Peru, Cuba, Chile, Argentina, and Venezuela.

Conclusions

These circumstances have led to a predictable situation. The Puerto Rican short story has been able to define itself as a genre, —that is, it has freed itself from the traditional confusion about its techniques, limitations, and possibilities, freeing itself, at the same time, from embarrassing non-literary connections. It has been the writers of the forties generation who have done the most to formulate this rigorous definition of the genre. Equipped with ample knowledge of the history, technical development, and stylistics of the modern Western short story, they established, both in their creative work and in their criticism, the concept of *short story* in its exact proportions. They set aside the lax, comfortable attitude which had made it possible to catalogue as a short story every short narration in prose—from the historical or folkloric legend and the disjointed lyric outpouring, to the pleasant sketch or "costumbrista" vignette. The modern short story as it develops and evolves— Guy de Maupassant, Poe, Chekhov, Gorki, Pirandello, Hemingway, Joyce, Faulkner, Sartre, Camus—has been broadening its expressive and thematic possibilities, but it has been simultaneously limiting itself as a genre; in other words, it has been creating its techniques and rules, as well as its stylistic modes, in accordance with its own formal growth, and also in accordance with the esthetic sensibility of each period.

We think that the student of Puerto Rican literature can today honestly affirm, without fear of such an affirmation's being criticized as provincial or chauvinistic, that the best expressions of the contemporary short story in Puerto Rico can compete, and in effect do compete, deservedly and decorously, with good examples of the genre in any literature of the Western world.

Appendix. Bibliography of English Translations[6]

Listed below are the English translations which have appeared of the works of the eight short story writers mentioned as representative of the forties generation in the preceding essay.

Abelardo Díaz Alfaro

"The Dogs." In Barbara Howes, ed. *The Eye of the Heart.* Indianapolis: Bobbs-Merrill, 1973.

"Josco." In Barbara Howes, ed. *From the Green Antilles.* New York: MacMillan, 1966.

"Josco." In Edward Spargo, ed. *Voices from the Bottom* (The Olive Book). Rhode Island: Jamestown, 1972.

"Peyo Mercé Teaches English." In María Teresa Babín and Stan Steiner, eds. *Borínquen: An Anthology of Puerto Rican Literature.* New York: Alfred A. Knopf, 1974.

José Luis González

"In the Bottom of the Lake There Is a Little Black Boy." In *New World Writing* (New York, 1958).

"The Letter" and "The Passage." In María Teresa Babín and Stan Steiner, eds. *Borínquen.* New York: Alfred A. Knopf, 1974.

René Marqués

"The Blue Kite." In *Americas* (Washington, D.C., May 1965).

"Death." In *Short Story International* (New York, Feb. 1965).

"Death." in G. R. Coulthard, ed. and tr. *Caribbean Literature. London: University of London Press, 1966.*

"Give Us This Day." In Darwin J. Flakoll and Claribel Algería, eds. and trs. New Voices of Hispanic America; An Anthology. Boston: Beacon, 1962.

The Oxcart. Charles Pilditch, tr. New York: Charles Scribner's Sons, 1969.

"Three Men by the River." In Edward Spargo, ed. *Voices from the Bottom* (The Brown Book). Rhode Island: Jamestown, 1972.

Pedro Juan Soto

Hot Land, Cold Season. Helen R. Lane, tr. New York: Dell, 1973.

"The Innocents." In Barbara Howes, ed. *From the Green Antilles*. New York: MacMillan, 1966.

Spiks. Victoria Ortiz, tr. New York: Monthly Review Press, 1974.

The Problem of Language in Puerto Rico

I. Twenty Years Later: Language, Politics, and Pedagogy

Mr. Cándido Oliveras, a distinguished Puerto Rican economist and planner, has been for some months Puerto Rico's Secretary of Public Education. He belongs to the powerful and influential annexationist wing of the government party. (Despite the synthesis theoretically brought about by the Commonwealth's "associated freedom" policy, conflict between the "North American" [that is, annexationist] and "Puerto Rican-ist" groups continues unabated.) Mr. Oliveras has to his credit a brilliant career as an administrator , and undoubtedly possesses the hallmarks of what North American sociologists describe as the organization man.

Mr. Oliveras' appointment disconcerted those circles interested in education, not so much because of the professional background of the new incumbent as because of the paradox created by his assimilationist or annexationist ideological tendencies. In effect, all the official talk about a genuinely "Puerto Rican" orientation in the education of the country did not jibe with the naming of Mr. Cándido Oliveras to carry out future educational policy. (The image of the "Puerto Rican man" was said to be the pedagogical goal after intense, extensive, and exhaustive investigations and reports by local and foreign educators.) Nevertheless, in keeping with the characteristic courtesy and good will of the Puerto Rican people, no voice was heard attacking the appointment, thus giving Mr. Oliveras the benefit of the doubt, as he deserved.

The country still is unaware of the details of the new Secretary's ac-

Author's note: Part I of this essay was published in *El Mundo* of San Juan, Aug. 16, 1960. Part II was published in *El Mundo* of San Juan, Jan. 26, 1963, and was reproduced in pamphlet form that same year by the Puerto Rican Nationalist Party, with the author's consent.

tions as administrator and organizer within his department, although one can imagine, given the incumbent's background as a planner and economist, that they have been fruitful. On the other hand, the press brings us official notice of his first, or at least most prominent and publicized, action as educator. That is what should now interest the Puerto Rican people.

As his first move in the role of educator, Mr. Oliveras has chosen out of the thousand and one grave and urgent educational problems, to concentrate on intensifying the teaching of English in the public schools. For a planner accustomed to establish a rigorous order of priorities for unresolved problems, an accusation of haste would be unthinkable. We have to believe that Mr. Oliveras, after a long, patient, and conscientious study, sincerely and honestly thinks that the teaching of English is the fundamental problem, and the most grave and urgent one faced by Puerto Rican education. If we doubt this, we would have to conclude that there are non-pedagogical motives for the unusual prominence he has given it.

No sensible Puerto Rican, genuinely interested in the education of the coming generations, can dissent from Mr. Oliveras in one aspect of his inaugural educative measure: the English language should be effectively taught in the public schools of Puerto Rico.

Clear Reasons

The reasons are clear. From the utilitarian point of view, English is today the principal business language. Since the United States is the dominating economic power in the Western world, English acts as an imperial language, a function fulfilled by Greek, Latin, French, Spanish, and, to a lesser degree, Portuguese, in different historical periods.

From the humanistic point of view, English, like any other foreign language, opens broader horizons to thought and to esthetic pleasure; its knowledge leads us, for example, to the study of two of the most interesting and richest literatures of the contemporary world, the English and the North American.

From the political point of view, we have the fact that, of the five Western languages spoken in America (Spanish, English, Portuguese, French, and Dutch) Spanish and English are the ones politically, geographically, historically, and culturally dominant in this hemisphere. The teaching of English as a preferred foreign language should be as obligatory in the public schools of the Latin American countries as that of Spanish in the public schools of the United States.

No matter what the political future of his country, the Puerto Rican should always have English at his disposal as one more cultural instrument of his historical condition as an American. Whether the United States be considered as friend, enemy, providential father, destructive Moloch, or mere "partner," there is no better way to understand and struggle with this collective entity than knowing the language in which it expresses its most intimate self. All this is simple, unadorned, logical, undeniable, and irrefutable.

Extreme Priority

However, there are two aspects of Mr. Oliveras' initial pedagogical measure which give rise to serious doubts and are in need of exhaustive discussion. On the one hand, we can question the criteria upon which he bases the decision to give highest priority to the teaching of English in our public schools. On the other hand, we can foresee that, intentionally or not, he will be encouraging by his action the pedagogically unsound practice of teaching all academic subjects in English. Moreover, those "privileged" groups who will "voluntarily" have their other subjects taught in English (with instruction given by North Americans) are going to constitute a minority with attitudes, ways of thinking, and patterns of conduct different from those of the bulk of the student body. Isn't this the same kind of divisive situation we have been warned against in regard to teaching religion in the public schools? We think it is, and we think that the social and psychological consequences are even more serious.

In one way or another, we find an abysmal lack of breadth and depth in this linguistic measure. The Secretary of Education merely reiterates in his plan the stereotyped and unrealistic palliative of "intensifying English." It has been shown over and over again that, due to the neglect which the base idiom or vernacular has always suffered, such a plan is doomed to the most blatant failure. And this is in spite of the wealth of expertise which has been focused on the matter and the many methodologies utilized.

We had agreed, or, to be exact, the best-known educators in the contemporary Western world had agreed, that in order to acquire an adequate command of a foreign language (be it the second, third, or fourth), the child must first have an adequate command of the vernacular, unless one is trying to destroy or eliminate the first language in order to impose the foreign one as the vernacular. The Secretary of Education knows that the Puerto Rican today—child or adult—is not even remotely close to having a command of his own language because of obvious faults in the very educational system which Mr. Oliveras today controls. The logic of the situation dictates that the first priority should be given to improving the teaching of Spanish, which has been shamefully neglected for decades. If this is the Secretary's intention, he has not produced a definite plan for it, as he has done in the case of English. This obviously makes one think that in Mr. Oliveras' mind the teaching of the vernacular is only secondary or subordinate to the teaching of what he calls a "second" language for the Puerto Rican. Pedagogically, of course, this is wrong.

An Escapist Way

To reduce the educational problem of teaching languages in Puerto Rico to the narrow cliché of "intensifying English" would be an escapist and unpedagogical way of NOT facing the crux of the question. One might even question whether the Secretary's plan were related to the teaching of languages at all. Moreover, are we to understand the new plans aim to "intensify the teaching of English" in a literally pedagogical sense? We very much fear that we are not.

Even less pedagogically acceptable is the opening which the Secretary of Education's plan has provided for the teaching of other academic subjects in English. The skill with which he talks around this fact cannot hide its existence. We had also agreed, or, to speak more exactly, well-known and prestigious North American and Puerto Rican educators had agreed, that the teaching of academic subjects in a language that is not the vernacular is not only illogical but dangerous. It is so much so that twenty years ago the Department of Public Education, after more than forty years of agonizing controversy, adopted instruction in the Spanish language as its official policy. It is very true that in the private schools, especially the Catholic ones, this regulation is constantly violated with the sufferance of successive Secretaries of Education (the official responsible for "recognizing" the private schools in Puerto Rico). In these schools instruction is given almost completely in English. But the violation of the rule by the private schools does not invalidate the official regulation itself. The new rule announced by the Secretary of Education does, however, contradict (and in practice and in the long run may invalidate) the educational policy recognized and adopted officially by the Government of Puerto Rico.

Finally, we cannot help but find a little inopportune the Secretary's recommendations with respect to the social imposition of English, in the schools as well as in the community, by means of audiovisual propaganda, clubs, debating teams, newspapers, and frequent personal contact of the students with the North American residents. His comments seem exaggerated and out of proportion because no system of public education, though its objectives may include the teaching of a language other than the vernacular, has reached such extremes and because Mr. Oliveras has not shown any official interest in encouraging the perfecting of our own language in such a spectacular way. We would have liked, purely in a spirit of pedagogical justice, for the present incumbent in Education to have felt as great an interest in his native tongue as he feels for English. We do not perceive this sense of elemental and logical justice in the rules Mr. Oliveras suggests. They are in fact discriminatory under the present circumstances. One deduces from them that the intention is not to make English a useful instrument, and a "second" language for the Puerto Rican, but to try to substitute it for the vernacular. The political implication of what is apparently being attempted is too obvious for us to insist upon it. It is, in the final analysis, not a matter of "intensifying the teaching of English" in Puerto Rico, as the Secretary of Education's press release euphemistically expresses it, but rather a new attempt, now on a large scale and with powerful backing, to supplant Spanish as the native tongue of the Puerto Ricans, replacing it with English. This political process will be carried out (as the Secretary himself stated) by the Department of Public Education, the University of Puerto Rico, and a committee of citizens in sympathy, naturally, with the intention of the plan.

The Same Crossroads

All of this places us at the same political-pedagogical crossroads which we thought we had passed twenty years ago. As if the things which today divide us were few, the "problem of language" will be yet another. We will have to become involved again (every one in accord with his own theories, criteria, and convictions) in the old and tiresome "battle of the language." Politics and pedagogy will again be mixed and shaken furiously in the public cocktail shaker and, as a consequence, pedagogy will suffer and politics will not gain anything appreciable. In the end, ironically, Puerto Ricans will continue speaking English as little and as badly as we do today, not only because of the slight pedagogical value of the new regulations, but because the inevitable public polemic will create in thousands of our children resistance to the language under question. It has happened before in Puerto Rico and it will happen again as many times as the same circumstances are repeated.

We therefore feel that Mr. Cándido Oliveras' first act of importance as Secretary of Public Education cannot be called a fortunate one.

Nevertheless, as characteristically courteous and considerate Puerto Ricans, we should continue giving the present Secretary the benefit of the doubt. It is possible that the linguistic plan conceived by him and his advisers may be less political and egoistic, more generous, humanistic, and pedagogical than was expressed in the extensive official press release issued by his office. It is always possible, moreover, that he and his advisers may feel inclined to correct the worst extremes of that plan before putting it into practice. For the benefit of the best and most effective teaching of the English language in Puerto Rico, a cultural problem which concerns us almost as much as Mr. Oliveras, we hope that this is so.

Appendix

1. On the first page of the August 30, 1960, edition of *El Mundo*—four days after the above piece was published in that newspaper—an article by the newspaperman Luis Sánchez Cappa appeared beneath the headline, OLIVERAS DECLARES SPANISH TO BE THE MEANS OF INSTRUCTION. The first three paragraphs are reproduced below:

> The Secretary of Public Education, Mr. Cándido Oliveras, affirmed yesterday that the "norms" of the Department as to the use of the Spanish language as the vehicle of instruction throughout the whole school system have not changed. He informed us that by the end of the month the recommendations that he would make to the Spanish Section of the Department "to strengthen the teaching of our vernacular language in the schools" would be ready.
>
> Although Mr. Oliveras does not mention it in his statement, they are in reply to an article published in *El Mundo* by the dramatist René Marqués which criticized certain aspects of the plan announced by Secretary Oliveras for intensifying the teaching of the English language in the public schools.
>
> Secretary Oliveras affirms that "during my incumbency the teaching of Spanish itself will be improved and intensified and the teaching of all subjects in Spanish will continue, which does not prevent the intensification and inprovement of the teaching of English as a second language and preferred subject."

2. Personal letter from the ex-educator and lawyer Mr. Francisco Vizcarrondo Morell to the Secretary of Public Education, Mr. Cándido Oliveras—with a copy to René Marqués—in relation to the problem set forth in "Language, Politics and Pedagogy." With the express authorization of Mr. Vizcarrondo Morell, his communication is reproduced

here because we think that it serves as a proper background to the problem, giving historical data and an additional perspective.

San Juan, Puerto Rico
August 20, 1960

The Honorable Cándido Oliveras
Secretary of Public Education
Santurce, Puerto Rico

Dear Mr. Secretary,

Expressing my best wishes for your success in the task of directing our educational system, I write to you in a constructive spirit of commentary and not of criticism concerning your recent statement about plans for the intensification of the teaching of English as a preferred subject and to clarify the comments offered by Mr. René Marqués.

I base my comments on my direct experience as teacher, principal, District Superintendent, General Superintendent and Secretary, and Head of the Technical Office of the Educational System from 1900 to 1920, and as Sub-Commissioner and Interim Commissioner and Head of the Technical Office of the System from 1920 to 1930. During this thirty-year period the essential concerns for the functioning and gradual development of our educational system were the question of the language of instruction, the preservation of the vernacular in all its purity, and the acquisition of English to the highest degree of perfection possible.

I received a new appointment during President Hoover's administration for 1930 to 1934, which I declined so as to begin my long-postponed (1917–30) practice as a lawyer-notary. I recommended Dr. Padín as my successor, and in 1935, with the extension of his appointment for a new term from 1935–39, the process of establishing the vernacular as the medium of instruction throughout the elementary school years was completed. It was not established through high school until after the untimely changes which took place in the years 1937–45. At the request of the Secretary of the Interior and of the then Head of the Territorial Division, Dr. Gruening, I intervened in Washington in 1939 concerning those changes, although I was then out of the department.

In 1945, the institutions invited to make a study of our educational system, especially as it concerned the medium of instruction, clearly upheld the use of the vernacular as the proper medium and the teaching of English as a preferred subject, and also established the fact that for a satisfactory study of English a solid knowledge of the native language is essential.

You know perfectly well that, owing to the exodus of thousands of good teachers over the last few years for justifiable economic reasons, our public school system has fallen to a very low level in general instruction, and especially in the teaching of Spanish and English. The recent gradual increase in the teachers' salaries will make it possible to keep the better teachers and to attract better students to the University's College of Education, and the task of rebuilding (entrusted to you) will take considerable professional effort over a period of time.

In summary, the fundamental program of the school system, as it is understood by you, should continue:

1st. The vernacular language should be the vehicle of instruction (without exceptions).

2nd. The teaching of SPANISH as a subject and as vehicle of instruction should merit preferential consideration.

3rd. The teaching of ENGLISH as a subject should also merit preferential consideration, without its affecting the preservation of the vernacular in all its purity.

4th. Our teachers should receive *special preparation* for the teaching of SPANISH and ENGLISH.

5th. The "Double Matriculation" and the "Alternate Matriculation" will be gradually eliminated in accordance with the economic resources available for the general functioning of the System.

Cordially yours,
Francisco Vizcarrondo Morell

3. A personal letter from René Marqués to Mr. Francisco Vizcarrondo Morell, with a copy to the Secretary of Education, Mr. Cándido Oliveras:

San Juan, Puerto Rico
August 24, 1960

Mr. Francisco Vizcarrondo Morell
Apartado Postal 1002
San Juan 5, Puerto Rico

Distinguished friend,

I am profoundly grateful for your kindness in sending me a copy of your communication to the Hon. Secretary of Public Education, in relation to the plan proposed by him concerning the intensification of the teaching of the English language.

It pleases me very much that I coincided in my fundamental points of view with the valuable judgement of an educator of your prestige and great experience. It is significant that individuals belonging to the different generations active today in Puerto Rico are in agreement about this cultural problem crucial to the Puerto Rican people. (You will have read, undoubtedly, the column *Hojas Libres* by the writer and professor Enrique A. Laguerre, published in today's edition of *El Mundo* [Wednesday, August 24]). Apparently the *preservation, intensive use,* and *perfecting* of the vernacular, together with an effective teaching of English, is one of the few but tremendously important objectives which brings together in agreement all those on this island interested in the development of a Puerto Rican civilization.

I am sure that, fundamentally, Mr. Cándido Oliveras, as Secretary of Education, also must agree with us. It is probable that the weaknesses or faults of his plan are due to inadequate advising, a reparable error as long as the guidelines announced by him have not yet been put into practice.

The trajectory which you indicate in the five points of your letter to the Hon. Secretary of Education seems to me to be one of elemental justice and of genuine pedagogical value. May I congratulate you for it?

Grateful for your kind attention, I remain,

> Very Cordially,
> René Marqués

4. Mr. Cándido Oliveras left the position of Secretary of Public Education at the end of 1964. The present incumbent—1966—is Dr. Angel Quintero Alfaro.

II. The Three Aspects of the Language Problem (Statements for the "Sociedad Obispo Arizmendi Pro Defensa del Idioma")

The problem of the preservation of the native language, and, as a corollary, of the teaching of Spanish in Puerto Rico, has three aspects—pedagogical, cultural, and political—which, given the conditions and circumstances of our people, are almost unavoidably intermingled.

Pedagogically speaking, it is a scientifically incontrovertible fact that students should be taught in their native tongue; it is not mere speculation or theory, but a fact corroborated by eminent European, North American, and Puerto Rican specialists in education, and proven by the educational experience of centuries, in different countries of the Western world, including, naturally, the United States of North America. It has never occurred to anyone—educator, politician, or private citizen—in a civilized and politically sovereign country to cast doubt on that pedagogical reality.

Only in those colonial countries where the native language is distinct from the language of the colonizing country does the conflict arise. In that situation education is utilized as a powerful tool of indoctrination and colonial domination. Pedagogy in this case is put in the service of politics, and loses its scientific character and its true social mission. Its legitimate aim of elevating the intellectual and spiritual level of the people whom it presumably serves is corrupted. Those who defend the foreign language at any cost are to be found then, logically, in that faction of imperialists and colonialists who either defend the status quo or aspire to a more humiliating subjection or to a more complete assimilation of the colonial people by the imperial power. It is thus natural that their arguments never have any scientific base. The reasons they brandish for destroying the active use of the native language are based not on pedagogical science but on political circumstance. This is precisely what has occurred in Puerto Rican society.

When a leader or citizen in favor of assimilation tries in Puerto Rico to refute the pedagogical reasons for teaching in the native language, he completely bypasses pedagogy. He speaks either of the economic "advantages" to be gotten from the foreign language or of the social "prestige" which it supposedly confers upon those who utilize it in the colony. In the first case, a purely materialistic value is attributed to the language of the metropolis, while in the second it is superstitiously granted almost magical attributes. On the one hand, the Puerto Rican who does not speak English is destined to "die of hunger" in his own Spanish-speaking country; on the other, the Puerto Rican who does not receive his instruction in the foreign language will remain always and fatally submerged in a state of social inferiority, condemned not to be able to "live decently" in the land of his own people. That is, in essence, the entire gamut of "objective" and "scientific" reasoning presented, in the pedagogical area, by the enemies of the vernacular within colonial Puerto Rican society.

In its cultural aspect, language, as it has been accepted by anthropologists, not only serves the purposes of communication but is a fundamental expression of culture itself. Even in the case of primitive peoples, the knowledge of the dialect of the tribal group is indispensable if one wishes to arrive at a complete knowledge and a full understanding of the indigenous culture with all the psychological and spiritual nuances and subtleties involved. When one ascends the scale of human knowledge— now on the philosophical plane—we have today a Heidegger who discovers in the *mother tongue* the raison d'être of his own being.

To attack the language of a people is therefore to attack the very roots of its personality, its most intimate spiritual expression, the very essence of its being. The very first step in the destruction of a culture and in the spiritual annihilation of a people is the impoverishment and, if possible, the destruction of its native language. Consciously or unconsciously, all the imperial powers of the Western world, including the United States, have recognized this and, as one of their methods of colonial domination, have imposed the learning of their language followed by the teaching in it.

Puerto Rican society during its sixty-four years under the North American regime has struggled stubbornly against this colonial reality. The United States has not accomplished its ultimate goal, though it has been able to count on all the necessary material support. It has made some progress, however. It has achieved a notable impoverishment in the expressive potentialities of the vernacular. Logically, in our country, there is an ambiguous, ambivalent situation, a pathetic intellectual, spiritual, and psychological confusion which has led, in large sectors of the population, to a weakening of the creative power of the word, of the language as an expressive medium, and even of the language in its communicative capacity. The supposedly "bilingual" Puerto Rican cannot, generally speaking, express his most inner self either in Spanish or in English. The moment is, then, crucial for the survival of the native tongue and, therefore, for our culture of Hispanic roots. Either the Puerto Rican people build today effective barriers against North American linguistic and cultural penetration or they risk losing their language and culture for future generations, not, now, in the event of a hypothetical future annexation, but within the present colonial reality.

The political element is implicit in the exploration of the first two aspects of the problem. While Puerto Rico continues being, as it is, the colony of a power with a language different from its own, the dilemma of the language can never have a *definitive* solution. Pedagogical policy on the matter—as our contemporary history has shown—will always be obliged to adapt itself to the ups and downs of colonial politics: now in favor, tomorrow against the native tongue; today Puerto Ricanist, tomorrow North Americanist in its defense of cultural values. The colonial situation offers no guarantee, for example, that the reasonable attitude of the present incumbent in the Public Education post will last. With sufficient pressure from the metropolis, Puerto Rico's educational policy will be obliged to change direction again in the usual fashion. Our experience as a colonial people has amply demonstrated this.

Therefore, it is possible to affirm that if those in favor of assimilation are ingenuous because they believe in good faith in the survival of Spanish and of Puerto Rican culture within the brusque and almost total absorption which federal statehood would imply, equally ingenuous and deluded are those in favor of the Commonwealth who believe, also in good faith, that they have the power and the ability to preserve their language and culture while faced with the slower but steady process already under way of assimilation and absorption within the present colonial situation.

Only by relying on the full and sovereign assurance that Puerto Ricans themselves, free from any foreign pressure, will decide on questions of such vital importance, can there be any surety that the problem of the preservation and the enrichment of the native language in Puerto Rico will be resolved, once and for all. Only the full enjoyment of national sovereignty will free the pedagogical problem from all extra-pedagogical adherences. Only political independence will make obsolete the tiresome battle which now robs us of so much spiritual energy, so much time, and so much potential for fruitful and creative action.

Appendix

In November 1965, two years after having published the above work, the author was invited to a conference of North American and Puerto Rican educators which was to take place during three days at the Hotel Barranquitas, on diverse educational problems which affected the Puerto Rican child. I was not able to attend the conference because I was working on the revision of the text, notes, and bibliography of this collection of essays. However, in the Sunday edition (November 21, 1965) of the *San Juan Star*, on page 3, there appeared an article about that conference of educators by the newspaperman Frank Ramos under the headline of U. S. SCORED ON LANGUAGE STAND HERE. The article deals with the subject treated in the two parts of the above essay, "The Problem of Language in Puerto Rico."

We produce below various passages from that newspaper article:

> Clarence Senior, member of the Council of Higher Education of the City of New York, attacked yesterday "the stupidity with

which the United States has treated the language problem in Puerto Rico."

Mr. Senior, a sociologist who has written several books about the island, told the conference of educators here yesterday that the Puerto Ricans were still trying to overcome the difficulties created by the insistence for many years of the United States government that English and not Spanish should be the vehicle for teaching in the schools.

Mr. Senior pointed out to the conference members that they had failed to work hard enough on the language problem in Puerto Rico, which is itself due to the "totally idiotic way in which, unfortunately, the United States has handled the educational system on the island." . . .

"What can one do with an imperialism which insists that its own language be imposed on conquered countries?" asked Mr. Senior.

In a later interview he said that the great majority of educators have urged that Spanish be the medium of instruction in Puerto Rican schools, with English being studied as a second language.

Mr. Senior attributed the educational policy of the United States to the tendency of many North Americans to consider as inferior, people (or countries) with customs and cultures different from their own.

He said that the attitude of the United States in relation to the language problem has been "an affront to the national dignity of the Puerto Rican people," as well as a bad policy from the pedagogical point of view.

We take pleasure in having reproduced the greater part of Mr. Clarence Senior's declarations, made in the 1965 conference of educators, since they reiterate what we said in "Language, Politics and Pedagogy" (1960) and in "The Three Aspects of the Language Problem" (1963). Since the colonial question continues to be a burning issue in 1965, it confirms what we said in our last study on this matter in 1963: the language problem in Puerto Rico cannot be *definitively resolved in favor of the native tongue* until the Puerto Rican people obtain complete power to rule their destiny and to resolve their own problems as a sovereign and independent nation.

A Character in Folklore and
a Theme of Farce in Puerto Rico

The folklore character Juan Bobo, the fool—that clumsy, awkward figure with a minimum of brains, a stuttering, harsh voice, enormous head, and pendulous lips—is not the Juan Bobo of this pantomime. I have attempted, rather, a re-creation of the character giving him traits more peculiar to the Puerto Rican.

My Juan, then, is a "fool"[1] because of his candor, his ingenuousness, and his childish enthusiasm for everything strange and novel. He does not exhibit the moronic traits which characterize the Juan Bobo of our folklore, and lead him to unconscious cruelty.

I would like to think that the protagonist of my pantomime is more genuinely Puerto Rican than the other. We, as a people, have always been characterized by our ingenuousness. Ever since the Europeans tricked our Indians with colored beads, we have succumbed to every political cock and bull story that has come our way, reflecting the good and bad intentions of all sorts of characters, both islanders and foreigners. And even today, in spite of our vaunted maturity and of our supposed democractic and cultural progress, if one scratches the veneer of the deceptive high standard of living, one can still find in the Puerto Rican the same candor exhibited by the Indian admiring a showy necklace of colored beads. It does not matter whether he is an intellectual trying to interpret our insular world or a farmer struggling to earn his daily bread.

In 1898, North Americanism was the fattest of the colored beads that we were tempted with by the invaders from the North. Later, in 1942, dedicated Puerto Ricans displaying doctorates from North American

Author's note: Prologue to the author's own work, *Juan Bobo y la Dama de Occidente* (a Puerto Rican pantomime for a Western ballet), published by Los Presentes, Mexico, 1956 (with drawings by Lorenzo Homar).

103

universities changed the bead's name and told us that it was called *universalism*. And now, this native dedication of purpose and the brilliant inventiveness of Europeans marvelously adapted to tropical colonialism combine to assure us that the colored bead's real name is simply *Westernism*. That is all well and good. The name may vary, but the colored bead which dazzled the Puerto Rican Juan Bobo remains the same: in 1898, 1942, or 1956. And the purpose behind the fat and shiny bead will remain one and the same, namely to un-Puerto Rican-ize the Puerto Rican.

In order to defend my theory of ingenuousness, I, as a Puerto Rican, also become ingenuous. And I take seriously here, in the farce of the pantomime, that new pretext which has been baptized as Westernism. But first, let us analyze it.

The active conflict between North Americanism and Puerto Ricanism is and always will be irreconcilable. No matter how great our ingenuousness may be, we cannot be made to swallow certain clichés. Puerto Rico, *bridge* between two cultures? *Link* between the two Americas? An experimental area where two antagonistic ways of life are *harmoniously fused?* We may be ingenuous, but not deluded. We are dealing with the stubborn collision of two nationalisms: one extreme (the North American), the other diluted daily by the thousand complexities of centuries of colonial experience or aggravated occasionally with sparks of desperate fanaticism (ours). There have been concessions on both sides, though more on one side than the other, of course, and, undoubtedly, diplomatic, economic, or political contrivances in moments of international crisis. The difficulty of finding a permanent solution for our colonial reality, more difficult in the economic and social than in the political sphere, can make us wish for the impossible. And this motivates those literary images which attempt to camouflage our complicated reality with an illusory optimism: "bridge," "link," and so forth.

None of this works. The *bridge* does not have foundations built of wood from the ausubo tree[2] but of cheap imported pine—the termites eat it. The *links* are not made of strong native cordage, but of northern fiber—the implacable climate of the tropics will rot them. Above and beyond termite-infested bridges and rotten links two well-defined nationalities, with firm foundations, face each other: the North American and the Puerto Rican. They could *live together* on the breadth of the American continent, but they will never fuse within the confines of our Puerto Rican territory. This conflict is alive and real and will remain so until a more or less distant future, since it will not cease immediately upon our obtaining political independence, as the contemporary history of Panama, Nicaragua, and Guatemala (to mention only the more obvious cases) proves.

Having once accepted the reality of that conflict under its true name in our contemporary history, where does the other concept come from? From what abysses of confusion have the colonialists of the latest stamp gotten the "conflict" Puerto Rican-ism versus Westernism? Are we perhaps the heirs of an oriental culture? Do we not form part of the Western world? Is an anti-Western Puerto Rican possible? How can Westernism, on the other hand, be anti-Puerto Rican? Is the national Cuban, French, Argentine, or German culture anti-Western?

This conflict, of course, only exists as a pretext to hide the other one. We are Westerners by virtue of our Puerto Rican nationality. We will only project what is ours (art, literature, thought) upon Western culture by starting out from our national roots. In order to probe deeply into the essence of Puerto Rico, elevating it to universal significance, neither narcissism nor a hypnotic obsession with our past is called for. Nor is it necessary, in order to acknowledge our responsibility to the West, to pulverize our Puerto Rican heritage, just so that we may disperse its particles blindly and irresponsibly in an unfamiliar nirvana artificially created by those who call themselves Westernists.

The confusion created by the Westernists confuses Juan Bobo. And in our disturbed surroundings we cannot permit even Juan Bobo to be confused by this artificial and malicious conflict. When the "conflict" is unmasked, will the politicians, overcome with pity, invent then another name for that same and indivisible colored bead? The question remains for now unanswered. For here we are dealing with pantomime, not dialogue.

Message of a Puerto Rican to the Writers and Artists of Peru

Distinguished friends of the Peruvian nation:

I am grateful for the honor conferred upon me by the Organizing Committee of this First Convention of the National Association of Peruvian Writers and Artists when they invited me, as a Puerto Rican, to convey a message to you. I wish to express my profound admiration and my enthusiastic good wishes. It is truly an achievement for a country of our America to bring together in one body its very individualistic creative artists and to do so within the society that gives them their raison d'être.

As we examine the practical and intelligent agenda of this first Convention, it becomes clear that, both on the material and on the spiritual plane, you are focusing accurately on the most disquieting problems for the creator, problems common to the writer and the artist in the whole of our America.

Freedom of Thought, Creation, and Expression

It is the Second Committee, however, which will consider the fundamental problem on the agenda, a problem which goes beyond the professional field of the writer and the artist and to the heart of a problem vital to every American. I refer, of course, to the *defense of the freedom of thought, creation, and expression.*

Today, precisely today, when the sorrow over what happened to *El Tiempo*,[1] in Colombia, is so close to us, this subject becomes of imminent concern, far beyond mere rhetoric. The defense of this fundamental freedom should be for us, the writers and artists of America, a

Author's note: Message sent to the Fire Convention of the National Association of Peruvian Writers and Artists, 1955. Reproduced in *Cuadernos Americanos,* no. 6 (Nov.-Dec. 1955; later publ. Mexico: Editorial Los Presentes, 1957).

matter of active and constant militancy. The attack of the forces of reaction upon freedom of expression is not always so dramatic as in the case of *La Prensa* of Buenos Aires, or so crudely obvious as in the case of *El Tiempo* of Bogotá. The attack is not always so blatant. Its more quiet and subtle forms affect literature and art more than they do the daily press. Besides, it is not always official censorship which restricts freedom of expression and creation. There is also a private form of censorship, masked in ethical and artistic criteria, which functions by refusing or arbitrarily mutilating newspaper and magazine articles, by denying certain works and specific authors access to publishing houses, by using religious proselytism to destroy artistic or literary movements, and by promoting criticism lacking in rigor and discipline. This narrow and partisan criticism perverts esthetic values in order to judge works and authors from a purely political point of view. Private censorship is for us doubly dangerous. It may coexist with official censorship, it can function comfortably under the protection of democratic and constitutional rights, and it is not found exclusively in those societies which live under a crude dictatorial regime. It is an underhanded censorship, without the stigma of the official, and is so subtle, at times, that we are scarcely aware of suffering its effects.

There are, as well, two other fundamental problems which America has not as yet definitively solved. One is expressed in the theme entrusted to the First Committee: *the position of the writer and the artist faced with national and universal problems.* The second does not appear on the agenda, although consciously or unconsciously it probably motivated the celebration of this Convention and the creation of the association which sponsors it. I refer to *the isolation of the writer and the artist in our society.*

Nationalism vs. Universalism

We have not been able to establish ourselves sufficiently well in our surroundings, to make it possible to project our creativity to the rest of the world. We are trapped between two extremes toward which we move indiscriminately without being able to find ourselves at any specific point along the way. Faced with external threats, we take refuge in sterile nationalism. Faced with nationalist asphyxiation, we escape toward a superficial and chimeric universalism. We would have been able to come to an understanding of our own surroundings in the past century if we had not had hanging over our heads a constant external threat: the sweeping economic and political power of the United States of North America. No one can achieve inner peace—and the wisdom,

tranquility, and objectivity necessary to judge one's own problems—
when there is a big stick ready to crush the head which is supposed to be
qualified to study and resolve these problems. Fleeing from the menace
of Washington, we have been rabidly nationalistic or ridiculously
universalist, fascists or Communists, and, on occasion, let us confess it,
more or less sincere, more or less hypocritical eulogists of that threatening Anglo-Saxon club. What we have not always been, I think, is
genuinely American. With very few exceptions, honorable ones, our
ideological positions and our intellectual and political movements have
ultimately been formed in response to events foreign to our authentic
circumstances. We have almost always acted in reaction to an external
circumstance, or to a circumstance apparently our own which, when
examined in depth, also turned out to have been a reaction to a latent
threat from outside.

It is time for this pathetic aimlessness of the Latin American intellectual to cease. It is time now to accept two plain facts: the inevi-
tability of the North American threat and the futility of taking refuge
from it—fleeing from it—in a sterile nationalism or a utopic
universalism. Nor should we take too seriously the easy solution suggested to us by José Figueres[2] in a series of articles published recently in
El Mundo of San Juan. With a new vocabulary which he has skillfully
employed since being proclaimed a model liberal and democrat,
Figueres offers the old and easy solution of servilely imitating the
United States. The President of Costa Rica suggests that our youth, if it
lacks ideals, grasp hold of those sanctioned by Washington, D.C. If we
are backward in the technical and material aspects of modern life, José
Figueres proposes that we copy word for word the North American
technical formulas. The solution is so easy that it had already occurred
to others before Mr. Figueres.

We Puerto Ricans have suffered this so-called "solution" for the last
fifty-seven years. This is not the time to set forth a balance sheet of the
current Puerto Rican situation. But if someone should say to you that
by following this formula Puerto Rico has finally solved its political,
economic, social, and cultural problems you can, without scruple, tell
this Puerto Rican or foreign colonialist to his face: *You lie!* Puerto Rico
has not found the solution to its destiny among the nations of either
America. It does not lie in José Figueres' formula, which is not new to
us, although every once in a while it is disguised in a different form, nor
in the embittered and terroristic nationalism of Pedro Albizu Campos,
who, in spite of his mistaken methods or, rather, the absence of method
in his course of action, has been useful in keeping awake a colonial

conscience too prone to sleep. Nor is it found in the Commonwealth—which has been up to now only another colonial attempt to reconcile the irreconcilable—nor much less in the ingenuous Westernizing doctrine concocted in our University by Chancellor Jaime Benítez. Like so many other nations in the contemporary world, the Puerto Ricans keep stumbling along: testing, experimenting, advancing in one direction only to quickly back up; talking about one route when we are following another; having recourse to various ideals which quiet the anguish of our national conscience; and being confused and thrown off the track even when most sure that we are on the path to our goal. We constantly try to reconcile the contradictions of our society: our illusory high standard of living, with the congenital poverty on which it is superimposed; the pleasure which we feel on obtaining material marvels through comfortable subsidies from Washington, with the shame which both the subsidies and the pleasure they produce cause us; the expressed desire for greater independence, with the efforts which we make day after day to become more inexorably dependent upon the colonial power; the display of an unrealistic program of industrialization, with the inescapable reality that we are and will be an essentially agricultural country; and the hurried implementation of imported pedagogical, political, sociological, philosophical, or economic formulas, with the reality of a nation whose idiosyncrasies and circumstances are different from those of the country where these formulas originate. What is to be done? We will not know with certainty until we have solved the problem of our national sovereignty. We Puerto Ricans must, however, search for a solution deep within ourselves even though our colonial condition makes that search more painful.

Lately, no one has expressed with greater clarity the terms of the problem, while pointing toward a possible solution, than Antenor Orrego in his essay "La circunstancia de la cultura americana," in *Cuadernos Americanos.* "We are being devoured by our surroundings," he says, "because we refuse to conquer the resistance they offer us, and we do not assimilate their aggression so as to transform it into a life and thought genuinely our own." Further on he again insists: "Our genuine surroundings are devouring us because we still do not wish to live profoundly from within our own selves, from within the most intimate depths of our historic roots. It is a mortal metaphysical aggression against the possibility of one's own being." It seems to me that Antenor Orrego's essay constructs a solid base from which one can serenely approach the conflict of nationalism versus universalism (or Westernism) in our America.

The Isolation of the Writer and the Artist

As to the second problem, *the isolation of the writer and the artist,* I will touch on it only briefly so as not to abuse your hospitality. The problem has two phases: the isolation of the creative artist within his own national environment, and the poor communication and infrequent contacts which, in practice, keep him isolated from works and authors of other Latin American countries.

In relation to the first phase, it is not worth our while to enter into the reasons some individuals invent to keep themselves apart from their social responsibilities: mistaken attitudes of snobbery, the cultivation of the out-of-date concept of the ivory tower, and the theory of art for art's sake carried to its most ridiculous extreme. The reasons which matter are those created by social and political forces, because it is they which affect externally, but inevitably, the majority of creative artists.

On the one hand, the totalitarian regimes, or the parties which aspire to put them in power, tend to isolate the creator for one of two reasons: because they consider him useful and demand that he render exclusive service to "the cause," or because they consider him dangerous and deny him all right to create freely. The so-called "party discipline" which restricts and limits the writer and the artist does not flourish, however, exclusively in totalitarian regimes. To a greater or lesser extent, through our own experiences or those of others, we are all familiar with this menace.

On the other hand, the isolation of the intellectual in democratic countries is becoming each day more severe. This is, perhaps, not yet so obvious in Spanish American democracies. But the problem is acute in the United States. We see there the paradox that one of the best-equipped intellectual minorities in the Western world exerts, nevertheless, no influence upon the government, and certainly none on the masses. One could justify the situation if that minority had kept itself apart from its immediate surroundings. This is certainly not true, however, in the specific case of literature. If anything characterizes current North American literature, especially the novel, short story, and theater, it is its genuine national roots. For several decades the North American writer has revealed with passionate sincerity his deep-seated concern for the people, life, and problems of his country. The conflict arises because true democratic principles have been corrupted. In order to make the "average" man aware that all men are equal before the law, he has been led to believe that no values exist which are not encompassed within his own moral and intellectual limits. It is repugnant to this false democratic spirit to admit to the existence of an intellectual elite, which, therefore, within these narrow criteria, comes to be considered as an irritating and useless caste. The creative artist in this democratic society is, then, sincerely and even passionately interested in his world and his people, and yet he is rejected by that world and that people, a rejection which can be expressed by profound scorn, by frank antagonism, or usually, by complete indifference. When a country suddenly suffers the fever of a not completely understood democratization (and we Puerto Ricans experienced this to excess during the decade from 1939 to 1949) terms such as *intellectual, man of letters,* and *artist* become a stigma for the individual within the society which he, himself, probably helped to reform.

The utilitarian ideal of capitalist democracy aggravates the problem. Since everything is measured and is appreciated in terms of dollars and cents, what escapes this common measurement is looked upon as dangerous contraband. The concept of "usefulness" shrinks so as to exclude everything which is not tangible or capable of yielding tangible profits. Naturally, if this ideal is accepted, the creator and the work of creation are perfectly useless to the efficient functioning of the democratic-capitalistic machine.

In order to demonstrate the degree of confusion which a country can reach during the most intense period of democratization, permit me to cite three examples which I consider symptomatic of Puerto Rican life in the last few years. In the forties a phrase became famous in certain of our circles. One of the founders of the Popular Democratic Party, then already in power, would always tell a person he suspected of being a man of letters or of possessing artistic inclinations to speak to him "in prose." The phrase reflects the prevalent attitude and characterizes marvelously that period of unbounded utilitarianism. To speak "in prose" was certainly the slogan of that decade. And although in later years those in official circles have tried to restrain the beast which they themselves set loose, its course is unimpeded. Only three years ago the Institute of Puerto Rican Literature, connected to the University and presided over by Jaime Benítez, gave one of the literature prizes to a book on banking systems, written IN ENGLISH, by an Italian American professor and edited by the University itself under the title *Money and Banking.* And more recently yet—only a few weeks separate us from the event—Chancellor Benítez, in a picturesque speech of welcome to our University students, had recourse to the Platonic recommendation that poets should be exiled from the ideal republic to indicate to the future citizens of the capitalist democracy that the University is a laboratory where only "scientific truth" is to be sought. Creative artists who directly or indirectly live within the orbit of influence of North American utilitarianism must be alert to this type of ingenuous exaggeration which disfigures and adulterates the essence of democracy, rejecting or scorning, more or less covertly, literary or artistic creation.

The second phase of the problem of isolation, the one due to poor communication and almost total lack of cultural exchange, is felt more keenly in a country with almost no press, no publishing house, and no consulates and embassies of its own, as is the case of Puerto Rico. It also affects, however, to a greater or lesser degree, all Latin American countries. We are, on the whole, more familiar with the latest European and North American art and literature than with what is being produced in the Latin American world. If official circles will not move to break this isolation, it is up to writers and artists to initiate the task because the problem affects them more directly than anyone else. And although the individual effort that the creative artist can make in this respect is always valuable, it is on organizations like the one you have founded that the greatest responsibility for Latin American rapprochement, on both the literary and the artistic plane, will rest. For this reason I place my most profound faith in this National Association of Peruvian Writers and Artists in the hopes that it will be an exemplary organization, not only achieving the objectives that it proposes within the national confines, but also serving as a stimulus to as yet unorganized creative artists in other countries, and as a vanguard of Latin American cultural exchange.

Wishing you the most unqualified success in the efforts of this, your first Convention, I remain,

Fraternally yours,
René Marqués

San Juan de Puerto Rico
August 25, 1955

The Function of the Puerto Rican Writer Today

I think, or I should say, I fear that on fundamental matters there will be little or no disagreement in this forum. And I say that I fear it because it would be academic to organize a public forum to discuss a theme on which there is general agreement—in other words, to polemicize about something which does not admit or provoke or require any polemics.

I am convinced that, if this very night we were to corner any Puerto Rican citizen in the street, regardless of his social or economic condition or his academic preparation, although taking for granted, of course, that his intelligence is not yet dulled by alcohol—it is too early for that—and that he does not suffer from congenital imbecility (or imbecility acquired from the crude propaganda of the daily press); if we corner him, I repeat, and if, at close range, we put to him the question: "What do you think should be the function of the Puerto Rican writer today?" his answer, with devastating logic, would be: "To write about present-day Puerto Rico" or "To write works which reflect the present moment in Puerto Rico", or, perhaps, more succinctly, "To write Puerto Rican works," taking for granted that if they are written in the present in one way or another they will have to reflect it. This "average" man, as the anonymous citizen whom we knew before as John Doe is called today in statistics, would be saying to us, without any great intellectual effort, philosophical theories, or sociological postulations, that the function of the Puerto Rican writer is not to be alienated from the reality in which he lives, but on the contrary to face up to the reality of that time and space which was allotted to him. As a writer, he

Author's note: Paper read by the author in a forum on the theme stated in the title which took place in the Ateno Puertorriqueño of San Juan on October 9, 1962. For the purpose of this work we understand "writer" to refer to the creative writer.

Translator's note: Published in *Cuadernos Americanos*, No. 2, March-April, 1963; reprint, 1963.

must observe its multiple contradictions so as to arrive at a profound truth.

It seems to me that neither the participants nor a substantial majority of the public present here would object to accepting in principle the validity of John Doe's opinion concerning the theme we are discussing tonight. Nevertheless, in the atmosphere of the Learned House, and unlike the man we cornered in the street, we have the mission, the obligation, and the duty—if not the function—to spin a finer thread.

I think it fitting, in the first place, to introduce some irritants into the discussion. Therefore, I am going to undertake a considerable detour before arriving at the specific theme of this evening. My friend the moderator will have the kindness to take me to task if the detour— speaking in sidereal terms—goes too far "out of orbit."

For paradoxical effect, let me begin that task of spinning more finely with a very gross platitude: The writer, be he Puerto Rican, Japanese, Russian, French, or Mexican, has as his primary function the creation of literature. If his creative gift is directed toward something other than creating literature, he will be precisely what the other thing is, but he will not be a writer.

If we accept the fact that literature is that genre among the products of human understanding which has for its goal the expression of the beautiful (or the esthetic expression of the ugly or even the horrible) by means of the word, we see clearly that the esthetic element is at the very root of literary creation, that is, of the function of the writer. To use a cliché, the writer is "the artist or the artificer of the word." The word in the hands of the writer is not, then, mere communication as it is for everyone else, but primarily, expression, esthetic expression.

The word thus serves two essential purposes, one utilitarian (communication) and the other esthetic (artistic expression). Any man, including the writer, naturally, *communicates* with others through daily conversation, correspondence, speeches, newspaper articles, pamphlets, the classroom, conferences, and forums. The writer as such, on the other hand, expresses himself to others through a work of literary creation. In both instances, that of communication and that of expression, the instrument is the same (the word), but the ends and the means are clearly distinct.

To what entity does this citizen whose function it is to create literature owe his first loyalty? Although it may shock many of you, I would like to affirm that, as a writer, he owes loyalty to no one but himself. And I do not make this apparently antisocial affirmation because of a childish desire to shock, but because of a firm conviction that this is so, and not in the way that many would like.

To be a writer is to undertake an agonizing and unending search for the truth. And it is not in outer space that the writer searches for the truth, but in man, in his fellow men, and in the society which surrounds him. But man, his fellow men, and society distrust or fear the truth and weave an intricate web of pseudo-truths and rigid dogmas which finally take shape in the state, and the state functions by means of a presumably miraculous cure-all which we will take the liberty of calling "the system."

The writer has to be free to be able to struggle against that web which others fashion to impede his search for the truth. And, in effect, he feels free, he knows himself to be free. This is a natural feeling, since he has the experience of creation; he knows, because he has experienced it in his own flesh and spirit, that the act of artistic creation is an act of supreme liberty, perhaps the freest of all the acts that man can execute. The writer, who knows freedom not as a political concept or as a philosophic abstraction, but as a vital experience, will love liberty for himself and, by extension, for others.

A free being who searches for the truth through esthetic expression, the writer becomes an ethical man. And, although he does not wish it and does it in spite of himself, he often becomes a moralist.

Now, what is the truth for which he anxiously searches? In the words of Ferrater Mora the truth was conceived by the Greeks "as the discovery of being, that is, as the vision of the form or profile of what truly is, but which is hidden by the veil of appearance." Millennia later, Heidegger returns to the Greek term of "discovery" or "unveiling" in referring to the truth. For him it becomes "an element of existence, which conceals being in its state of degradation and discovers it in its state of authenticity."

The writer, of course, does not have to be up on the different philosophical interpretations of the truth, although it wouldn't hurt him to acquaint himself with some of them. What is important to point out is that his personal and intuitive search for truth always carries with it that dramatic element of "discovery" or "unveiling." An essential part of his labor, if not the very essence of his never-ending search, is to break through the surface appearances, to bring to light what is true, and to rip away the veils which conceal the authentic.

It is very easy for the rest of humanity to find *their* truth, or at least to hold the naive illusion that they have found it. There are even many who say they have found the absolute truth. (We use the phrase not in the rigorous philosophic sense, but in that of a presumably unquestionable truth.) The politician and the man of religion, among others, assure us that they possess it. But for the writer there are no absolute truths.[1] As soon as he learns what he believes as a writer to be the truth, he discovers that it is only a part of the truth, a half truth, or a reflection of the truth, or only a mirage. The absolute truth is not there; it is somewhere else. He must begin again his tireless search.

Do you understand now why the writer always seems to be eternal nonconformist? Do you understand why his loyalty to governments, states, political parties, religious doctrines, institutions, and systems is almost always relative and conditional; why he so often has to feel, in reality, loyal only to himself? Do you understand why, faced with the rigid and dogmatic truths of the State, the Church, or Society, the writer almost always appears as a rebel, as a heretic, or even a subversive?[2]

It is obvious that the writer will always identify himself with libertarian causes, because freedom is a necessity for one who creates. Furthermore, his ethical sense and his moralistic inclination will cause him to identify with revolutionary causes, since he will inevitably see in them reason and justice. Still, one should not be fooled. Save for such brilliant exceptions as a José Martí, the writer will never be a liberator or a revolutionary. He can, in a crucial moment in the life of his country, change his pen for a rifle, becoming a soldier or a guerrilla, or he can temporarily sacrifice expression for communication, becoming a mere pamphleteer. When the crisis is past, however, and the cause with which he has identified and for which he would fight is saved, he will again become, as a writer, faithful to himself. He will return to his uncomfortable position of eternal rebel unless, of course, he ceases being a creator, unless the man of action within him is able to destroy the writer. Barring this, he cannot avoid being in some measure a rebel within the new system, as he was within the system which he helped destroy, since in both he sees the inevitable contradictions.

He will be a rebel in the Camusian sense—in disagreement with the status quo and a critic of it. If the moment arrives, he will be its declared enemy, but incapable of formulating a system to substitute for the one he condemns. The revolutionary, on the other hand, is the one who has clearly formulated the system which is to replace the one he destroys. He possesses a truth which he believes absolute. The writer is incapable of such a feat, though he may at times delude himself.

We are seeing why it is practically impossible to demand solutions from a writer. He perceives, discovers, sets forth, and denounces contradictions and problems—contradictions and problems which generally were passed unnoticed by others—but he does not give solutions. He can point out various possible solutions because he sees in each one of them a little truth, but none by itself seems to him as the absolute and true solution. If it should occur to him—and this has happened— to try to synthesize what he thinks the best of all these possibilities, the result would be an ideal impossible to put into practice in the everyday world—in short, a utopia. It falls to the man of action, to the politician, to realize the synthesis, to give the practical solution, to state the new truth with all its contradictions. These contradictions will create new problems in the future to be discovered and denounced by other writers and solved by future men of action, thus continuing, ad infinitum, the inexorable cyclical process.

In relation to what we have said, we should examine a phrase very commonly used today: "revolutionary writer." This term is applied indiscriminately to the writer who, in a given moment, has taken up arms to fight in a revolution and to the one who has incorporated in his work revolutionary episodes and events, but it is a more common practice to designate in this way the writer who inhibits his creative freedom to keep his work within the rigid ideological directives of a government party which rose to power by means of a revolution: the directives of the state, in other words.[3]

The term "revolutionary" applied to the writer in this sense is, of course, absurd. The writer, as such, is only revolutionary if he brings a "revolution"—that is, a fundamental change—to literary creation. Dante, Cervantes, Shakespeare, Pushkin, Dostoevski, Kafka, Proust, James Joyce, and Virginia Woolf were revolutionaries. Pablo Neruda was a revolutionary poet long before becoming a Communist. Significantly, the more Communist he has become, the less revolutionary poet he has been. Jean Paul Sartre is a revolutionary writer, in spite of his political inconstancy. His literary production is as revolutionary when he is within the Communist Party as when he is out of it, when he is praised by the Communists as when he is reviled by them. Sartre is a revolutionary writer, not because of his political activity in the French resistance, nor because of his periodic rapprochements with Communism, but because he achieves what always appeared extremely difficult, if not impossible: the writing of excellent literature with a philosophic doctrine. *The Flies, No Exit,* and *Nausea* have done more to disseminate and make understandable Sartrean existentialism than his confused and contradictory *Being and Nothingness.* That is so only because *The Flies* and *No Exit* are two excellent dramatic works and *Nausea* a good novel. It is the esthetic and human value of these literary works which sustains them as such. As a revolutionary writer Sartre has never betrayed himself, even when the citizen Jean Paul Sartre may have appeared a traitor to a revolutionary political ideology. Sartre, in my judgment, has fulfilled his function as a writer with integrity and in very difficult circumstances.

We can now, after this long detour, return to Puerto Rico and to the specific theme of this forum: the function of the Puerto Rican writer today. I imagine that we have all interpreted "function" in its social aspect. I think that that function does not escape anyone's notice. Puerto Rico has been for centuries and still is a colony. The fundamental problem of a person in a colonial situation is freedom. The writer, a lover of freedom because of his very condition as a creator, and inhabitant of a colony, will naturally identify with every movement of political emancipation. This, in our case, is not a mere theory, or an unrealized desire, but historic fact. The Puerto Rican writer was separatist in the times of Spain, as he is today a nationalist or an "independentista." His work reflects today, as it did yesterday, the colonial situation of his country. And his painful search for truth becomes one for freedom. Freedom is for the Puerto Rican writer the truth always sought and never captured. It is, therefore, the theme most repeated in Puerto Rican literature—the primary theme, I would venture to say. Whether it has a political thrust or deals with individual or metaphysical freedom, the Puerto Rican writer's desire for freedom is always present in his work. It is there not because of state imposition, nor because of party discipline, nor because of ideological directives, but because he has freely chosen this theme, one which is eternal and of the moment, for his creative work. He thus fulfills, in his free act of creation, his function as a writer in the time and space allotted to him: the colonial Puerto Rico of yesterday and today.

It only remains for me to add an observation and a warning with respect to the theme. The first is that the Puerto Rican writer, because of personal limitations, or because of the lack of a real vocation, or because he has deviated from his fundamental function, has often neglected the esthetic aspect of his craft. He has tried to be a writer using the word as his instrument, but more as a utilitarian means of communication than as a means of artistic expression. This is not a problem exclusive to Puerto Rico, but one of all Latin America. For obvious reasons, it has been the poet among us who first has been able to overcome that limitation. The problem is still visible in the prose writers, although we have to admit that, in Puerto Rico as well as in the other Latin countries of the hemisphere, there has been a great improvement in this respect over the last few decades. The Puerto Rican writer must be fully aware of this limitation, because it constitutes his major problem today. In terms of rigorous priority, the esthetic function precedes the social function. The writer has to be first an artist and then what he may choose to be or what suits his temperament best: politician, sociologist, moralist, philosopher, or metaphysician. The higher its esthetic value, the better a work will fulfill its social function; the greater its artistic values are, the wider dissemination and acceptance its content will have. Given a propagandistic work and a work of authentic literary value with the same content, the genuinely literary work will fulfill its social function more effectively and completely than the pamphlet. This is not a theory or an intellectual elaboration but a fact corroborated by millennia of literary history.

As to the warning, I feel it my responsibility to say that the Puerto Rican writer should already be preparing himself to face the not very distant time when the ideal truth so sought after by him and not yet captured will finally become reality.

Puerto Rico will be free. Because of historical imperatives the event will take place in the course of the present generation. The Puerto Rican writer, who has a long tradition of having liberty as his ultimate goal, is going to feel disconcerted before the apparently unaccustomed fact of independence. He is going to think, for a moment, that he has been able to seize hold definitively of the truth. He is even going to have the fleeting illusion that he finally finds himself before an absolute truth. But after independence there will come, in the political field, another truth to be achieved: national liberation. This will not be an absolute truth either, although it will be proclaimed as such at that time. There will never be absolute truths for the writer if he wants to fulfill, honestly and completely, not only his esthetic but his social function. He will always have a reality to examine, contradictions to discover, problems to denounce, and a more profound truth to capture. It is about this reality that I wish to caution the Puerto Rican writer of today, and of tomorrow.

Notes

Translator's Introduction

1. "La Literatura Es Fuego," *Mundo Nuevo*, 17 (1967), 94.

2. Juan Angel Silén, *We, the Puerto Rican People: A Story of Oppression and Resistance*, tr. Cedric Belfrage (New York: Monthly Review Press, 1971), p. 42.

3. Tomás Blanco, *Prontuario Histórico de Puerto Rico* (San Juan: Instituto de Cultura Puertorriqueña, 1970), pp. 128, 135.

4. Manuel Maldonado Denis, *Puerto Rico: Mito y realidad* (Barcelona: Ediciones Península, 1969), p. 47.

5. *Comentarios a un Ensayo sobre Puerto Rico* (San Juan: Ediciones Ateneo Puertorriqueño, 1964), p. 29.

6. Manuel Maldonado Denis, *Puerto Rico: A Socio-Historic Interpretation*, tr. Elena Vialo (New York: Random House, 1972), p. 230.

7. Silén, pp. 36-45.

8. "A Critical Look at Puerto Rico," *The San Juan Star*, Feb. 19, 1960, pp. 1, 25.

9. Silén, pp. 19, 45.

10. Northrop Frye, *The Stubborn Structure* (Ithaca: Cornell University Press, 1970), p. 20.

Literary Pessimism and Political Optimism

1. For an interesting and little known study of philosophic pessimism in the past century, see *El Pesimismo en el Siglo XIX* by E. Caró, member of the French Academy (Madrid: La España Moderna).

2. José Ferrater Mora, *Diccionario de Filosofía* (Editorial Sudameriana).

3. Francisco Manrique Cabrera, *Historia de la Literature Puertorriqueña* New York: Las Américas, 1956). In relation to the polemic about naturalism Dr. Cabrera directs the reader to a series of articles which appeared in the *Boletin Mercantil* Dec.-Feb. 1889-90).

4. North American pedagogical optimism has not so much elevated the masses as made all society equally mediocre. Individual conformism and social apathy are the result. See a serious and responsible study of this phenomenon in William H. Whyte's *The Organization Man* (New York: Simon and Schuster, 1956).

5. The concept that individual happiness might be distinct from that elaborated by the state or society does not enter into the optimistic calculations of the Russian or the

North American. This leads logically to the appearance of political "heretics" or "deviates" in Russia and of the "socially maladjusted" in the United States.

6. This was not an exclusively University phenomenon in those years. With the drastic solution to the university conflict in 1948, a pathetic era of silence began in Puerto Rico, lasting until 1952, the year the Commonwealth was proclaimed. Although the law guaranteed freedom of expression, the people maintained a distrustful silence, impressed perhaps by the absolute power of the government and by the aggressiveness of the Governor (Luis Muñoz Marin), who monopolized all political initiative even within his own party. Even the fleeting uproar caused by the Nationalist machineguns (October 1950) could not disturb this significant silence. On the contrary, it became even more hermetic. It was in those years of democratic apathy, shared by the people and the intellectual class and which coincided with "Macarthyism" and "witchhunting" in the United States, that one finds the cause of the accusations of "dictator" and "totalitarian state" which later were to be hurled at the Governor and his government. The accusation is false in a juridical sense (it was precisely during those years that the Independence Party began to participate in the elections), but it has subtle psychological justifications.

7. Nathan Koenig, *A Comprehensive Agricultural Program for Puerto Rico* (United States Department of Agriculture, 1953).

8. The *Roper Report,* inaccessible to the public because it has been kept up until now, November 1966, in government files as a confidential document.

9. Daniel J. Boorstin, "Self-Discovery in Puerto Rico," *Yale Review,* 45, no. 2 (Dec. 1955), 229-45.

10. *Translator's note:* The official name in Spanish of the Commonwealth of Puerto Rico is Estado Libre Asociado, which is literally translated as Free Associated State.

11. We, on our part, also discover something. For the first time frankly cynical attitudes and characters appear in Puerto Rican literature. And this almost always happens when the writer is dealing with local political themes. We interpret the phenomenon as a reaction to the cynicism latent in various of the new political postulates (we need only remember "associated freedom" to understand what we are referring to). We also see it as a denunciation of new collective attitudes which reveal to what degree the cynicism implicit in the most notorious official statements of the last years has permeated the masses. One example of these attitudes would be the frantic and desperate acquisition of material goods *at any cost,* cynically called a "realistic policy."

12. "Hora Teatral," WIPR-TV, March 29, 1958, 7:00 p.m.

13. We ask ourselves who truly was *sleeping:* the world or the author of the novel.

14. It will take just a few words to show how much artificiality there is in the "conflict." Superficial deviations in political tactics, possible personal disagreements or rivalry between the two functionaries, cannot hide the simple truth: the Chancellor and the Governor are twin branches of the same ideological trunk. It would not be necessary to probe very far to discover that the Chancellor Jaime Benítez is ideologically more similar to the Luis Muñoz Marín than the Governor is to himself. The former, as an intellectual, has been able to be faithful to the specific ideological posture (a frankly colonial annexationist one in this case). The latter, on the other hand, has not been able to escape the fatal chameleon-like talent which characterizes every man of action, especially when he holds political power in the ambivalent society of a colony.

15. The "housecleaning" has so far gone no higher than the municipal political level.

16. *Translator's note:* The word we have translated as "meeting ground" is *batey.* Marqués uses it ironically since it is an Indian word which Muñoz Marín popularized when he so described his chats with the people.

17. The origins of this attempt at state interference go back to 1938, when Jaime Benítez, then an official spokesman of the party now in power, gave a lecture at the University entitled "Luis Palés' Matos y el Pesimismo en Puerto Rico." Twelve years later this same lecture would serve as prologue to Palés *Tuntún de Pasa y Grifería* (San Juan: Biblioteca de Autores Puertorriqueños, 1950). One can already infer from the 1938 lecture of the then "enfant terrible" of the Popular Democratic Party (now perennial chancellor of the Colonial University) the "optimistic" thesis which the Government party is to adopt as its own and which the Governor will then attempt to project into all spheres of Puerto Rican life. Unfortunately, as much for the optimistic author of the lecture as for the no less optimistic Governor, the prophecy that pessimism in Puerto Rican literature would come to an end in 1938 never became a reality.

18. The Governor has passed his sixtieth birthday, which makes it, if not impossible, at least improbable that he will stay in power for the full period of the next twenty years. (This note was written in 1958. Today, in 1966, the ex-governor Luis Muñoz Marín is sixty-eight years old. He was born, significantly, in 1898, the year of the North American invasion.)

19. Those Puerto Ricans who have not yet lost their memories will be able to recall how many times over the last twenty years the official spokesmen have used the "backward" Latin American countries as a "living" example of what the "republic" would bring to the people in terms of hunger, barbarism, disorders, violence, crimes, and political backwardness. Those who keep their retentive faculties in a healthy state will not have forgotten either the Governor's insistent attempts, for years, to discredit concepts such as "independence," "country," and "freedom," which he jokingly (or seriously, perhaps?) called "obsolete." Today, when those in official circles claim to rejoice in the triumph of Fidel Castro's peasants, they should realize that those bearded Cubans are the embodiment of all the epithets which they, in Puerto Rico, consider denigrating: "patriots," "dreamers," "liberators," "idealists," "romantics." How those Puerto Ricans must have to salve their consciences in order to be able to praise as a virtue in Cuba the same things they are ready to revile in their own country! (For evidence of the turnabout of these Puerto Ricans with respect to Cuba see, in this book, "The Docile Puerto Rican.")

20. One can add to the growth of the minority Statehood Party (pro-annexationist) a significant fact: most present Cabinet members as well as other high government functionaries whose appointments come directly from the Governor belong to the annexationist wing of the party in power. The Governor has maneuvered so as to relegate the weak pseudo-"independentista" wing of his party to the legislative branch, which he dominates from his desk in Fortaleza, in spite of all the ostentatious democratic camouflage. Faced with the impossibility of the free exercise of the legislative function, the disoriented representatives and senators, if they feel enough sense of responsibility to examine the projects submitted by the Administration, must rely on the advice of the technical experts who write up those projects, specialists who are either the secretaries of departments or the directors of agencies, all sympathetic to annexationism, or their closest and most faithful subordinates. If we realize, moreover, that the University of Puerto Rico, the institution which is crucial in the ideological preparation of the next generations, is also in the hands of a skillful assimilationist, we are able to see clearly not only the present situation but what the future holds. That fiery revolutionary leader who was going to save the country from the old annexationist coalition as the thirties came to an end, today, after twenty years of "revolutionary" effort, can be seen delivering the country into the hands of the supporters of that same ideology from which, presumably, he was to

save it. There must have been few times in the history of a colony when the political labors of almost a quarter of a century have been as sterile as in this pathetic case of Puerto Rico.

21. The expert eye of the sociologist could discover in our society symptoms which limit our horizons more severely than ever. The shocking breakdown of moral and ethical values in a moment of great economic prosperity, the cynicism found not only in the older generation but also, unfortunately and markedly, in the youngest groups, and the frightful intellectual and spiritual confusion of the Puerto Rican when pressured from all sides to give unquestioning support to the maintenance of the status quo, are revealing signs of how traditional defenses have broken down. These are defenses which the Puerto Rican people had maintained for centuries in order to preserve their collective personality and integrity. It is likely that the essence of Puerto Rican being has never been in greater danger than it is today. Never had the colony been able to make of the Puerto Rican such a genuinely colonialist being as he is today. (His own blindness to this fact is proof enough that the fact exists.) Before, it was always possible to perceive potential resources in the Puerto Rican people with which to combat the economic and political colonialism but today the most qualified team of sociologists, anthropologists, and psychologists would have to probe very deeply to find potential strengths which could be used in the struggle against the moral and spiritual colonialism which is developing so shamelessly within Puerto Rican society.

22. *Los Casos de Ignacio y Santiago*, Libros para el Pueblo Numéro Cinco (San Juan: División de Educación de la Comunidad, 1953).

23. The study, which was concluded in 1955, had not yet been published. Nevertheless, the inferences from the analysis as it relates to what is expressed here were examined in René Marqués' article: "Writing for a Community Education Programme," published by UNESCO in *Reports and Papers on Mass Communication*, no. 24 (Paris, Nov. 1957).

24. Think about the parallel between the North American and Puerto Rican economic booms (the cause, presumably, of the optimism) and the acute pessimism in the literature of both countries.

25. The recent case of the writer Pasternak in Russia illustrates perfectly what we are saying.

26. Add to this the cathartic ending which, since the time of the Greeks, the West has attributed to tragic literature.

The Sound and the Fury of Mr. Kazin's Critics

1. See "The Docile Puerto Rican," in this book, an essay written after this one.

2. As this book goes to press (toward the end of 1965), there is a piece of news which may turn out to be partially or moderately encouraging. The Department of Public Education has included in a Special High School Program, a program for outstanding students at the pre-university level, a more intensive and extensive study of Puerto Rican literature, with future plans for a year course on the History of Puerto Rico. We will have to wait several years to see whether the project will go beyond the more or less experimental stage and be put in general use or whether it will stagnate or be discontinued as has happened to so many others in the unstable record of the Department of Education's curricula of the past twenty-five years. (Without taking away from the importance nor much less from the merit of the new project, one must point out that the terms it has been necessary to use to describe it are somewhat embarrassing: "experimental," "special program," "outstanding students," "future plans," etc. What in any free country in the world is a pedagogically sound, normal, and traditional element in public education, here,

and at this juncture, must be done timidly and cautiously, in an experimental, special, and, to a great extent, exclusive way! May the gods of pedagogy, including that good-natured Dewey and the so badly interpreted Ortega, protect the efforts of these daring educators who are trying to put *something* Puerto Rican on a level somewhat equal to "Western" things!)

3. Now (1966) nothing less than the president of the State University Centers, the supreme arbitrer of higher education—public education—in Puerto Rico.

The Docile Puerto Rican: Literature and Psychological Reality

1. V. García de Diego, *Dicconario Etimológico Español e Hispánico.*

2. Sainz de Robles, *Diccionario de Sinónimos y Antónimos.*

3. Roque Barcia, *Gran Diccionario de Sinónimos Castellanos.*

4. Since the present study is not a literary critique, it will allude to works not because of their esthetic value, but because of their theme or their psychological insight.

5. Kazin's article, published originally in the magazine *Commentary*, was reproduced by the local newspaper, the *San Juan Star*, in two consecutive editions (Feb. 19 and 20, 1960), under the title "A Critical Look at Puerto Rico."

6. We think it would be of great interest for the social scientist to carry out an intense and thorough study of the colony of North American residents in Puerto Rico. The ways of thinking, attitudes, and behavior of these people, who for the most part never or only precariously adapt to the Puerto Rican cultural structure, are a rich quarry for sociological exploration. Some of the so-called Puerto Rican problems, sociopolitical as well as psychological, could be clarified and better understood in the light of the results of such a study. Writers and journalists, without technical apparatus, have attempted several impressionistic studies of this type. Nevertheless, from the strictly scientific point of view, the field is virgin. It is of primary importance that it be explored, if we are to reach a complete understanding of present-day Puerto Rico.

7. The North American critic has confessed to me that he was not aware when he wrote his article that Puerto Rico had a national literature.

8. Crushed, in a moral sense; submissive.

9. Squatting, in a spiritual sense. (Both terms, linguistic inventions of the Puerto Rican when he still permitted himself the luxury of self-knowledge, are, in themselves, revealing of his psychology.

10. Antonio S. Pedreira, *Insularismo* (1st ed.; Madrid: Tipografía Artística, 1934).

11. *The San Juan Star*, Tuesday, March 8, 1960. The article of ours to which we refer was sent to the editor of the newspaper with its own title: "The Sound and the Fury of Mr. Kazin's Critics." For reasons difficult to determine—perhaps in order to give a "newsy" tone to the article—it was entitled on the first page, "Noted Writer Looks at Kazin's Content" and its continuation on the inside pages appeared as "Marqués Analyzes Kazin Content," which constitutes a nice problem for the bibliographer. (The article deals with the historical and political-cultural causes of Puerto Rican docility. So as not to be repetitious, we have not included them in this essay. The article, however, can be found earlier in this volume under the title, "The Sound and the Fury of Mr. Kazin's Critics."

12. *Asomante*, no. 3 (1956).

13. René Marqués, *Otro Día Nuestro* (San Juan: Imprenta Venezuela, 1955).

14. *Ibid.*

15. See the prologue to the anthology *Cuentos Puertorriqueños de Hoy* (San Juan:

Club del Libro de Puerto Rico, 1959). *Translator's note:* It is included in this volume under the title "The Puerto Rican Short Story of the Forties Generation."

16. United Nations, *Demographic Yearbook, 1951.* One can discover recent official attempts to sugar-coat this pill by assuring us that such facts are already out of date. In fact, Eric Fromm was invited last year to study suicide in Puerto Rico, and with exemplary politeness the hosts hastened to inform their future guest publically that the situation had gotten considerably better. We do not know if Fromm accepted the invitation, but we hope that, if he agrees to do the study, he takes two facts into consideration: the decline in population growth in Puerto Rico and the emigration to the United States, a tide that carries with it a considerable number of those social classes most susceptible to expressing their self-destructive impulses in literal or physical suicide. Any contemporary study would be more truthful if it were to include the emigrant Puerto Rican population with less than five years of residence in the United States, that is to say, the group which still conserves its psychological links to the homeland. Fromm, like a good psychologist, will also be sure to examine two questions which already concern some Puerto Rican psychiatrists: Is the high and ever-growing incidence of automobile accidents in Puerto Rico— against which neither the sanctions of the law nor the so-called civic educational campaigns help—one more manifestation of the Puerto Rican's self-destructive impulse? Is this Puerto Rican madness at the steering wheel which so astounds and alarms the foreigner, in the last analysis, a clear symptom of a suicidal tendency? Personally, we think so. (Now, in 1966, we can state that Eric Fromm never carried out that study under the auspices of the Puerto Rican Government.)

17. Pedro Juan Soto, *Spiks* (Mexico: Los Presentes, 1956); Emilio Díaz Valcárcel, *El Asedio* (Mexico: Editorial Arrecife, 1958).

18. This analysis of the suicidal tendency in its Nationalist manifestation cannot conceal nor even detract from the importance of Nationalism in contemporary Puerto Rican political history. When one views the phenomenon from a historical perspective, it can be seen that the immediate failure of Nationalism in its years of greatest activity was compensated for by its decisive and determining influence on all political activity after the decade of the thirties. As a defensive reaction, neither local colonial politics nor those of Washington failed to take into account the existence of the Nationalist movement. One can state that, in good measure, the colonial reforms granted in block under the name of the Commonwealth are the result of this reaction. One of the decisive cards played in Washington to hasten the approval of the new formula was the political threat, still latent at that time, posed by the Puerto Rican Nationalist Party. This makes one think that if Nationalist terrorism had been effective in the key years of their activity, it would have achieved the political objective which was the basis of their ideology. One can observe, as well, that in spite of the campaign of the last twenty years to defame and discredit it, of the official persecution and reprisals, of the disappearance of the Nationalists as an active political group, of the pragmatic, materialistic, and utilitarian attitudes which are fostered in our young people, and of the social atmosphere hostile to that ideology, it still holds a fascination for school and university groups. Apparently, then, one can be sure, up to a certain point, of its survival in the new generations. This is natural, since the fascination which Nationalism holds for the Puerto Rican is perhaps more psychological than ideological. There will always be Puerto Ricans, who, just because they are Puerto Ricans, will feel they must assume the collective guilt complex, thus aggravating to the hilt their self-destructive impulses.

19. The dates given in the text refer to the first staging of the plays.

Palm Sunday, staged; not yet published. *Encrucijada, Teatro Puertorriqueño* (San

Juan: Instituto de Cultura Puertorriqueña, 1959). *El Final de la Calle,* staged; not yet published. *Un Niño Azul Para Esa Sombra* in René Marqués, *Teatro* (Mexico: Editorial Arrecife, 1959). *Le Ceiba en el Tiesto* (San Juan: Biblioteca de Autores Puertorriqueños, 1956). *Los Derrotados* (Mexico: Los Presentes, 1956). *El Gigante* (Barcelona: Ediciones Rumbos, 1959).

20. Subsequent to this essay (written in 1960), Pedro Albizu Campos died in San Juan on April 21, 1965. Thousands of persons of all ideologies and economic and social classes filed by his coffin lying in state in the Ateneo Puertorriqueño. According to the calculations of the North American press in San Juan, sixty thousand Puerto Ricans came to his funeral, the largest and most impressive in the history of Puerto Rico. Thus, they paid posthumous tribute to the man who dedicated and sacrificed the major part of his life to the greatest and noblest ideal a country may have; its national independence. After the funeral honors in the Cathedral and in the very old and historic Church of San José, bombarded by the North Americans in 1898, he was buried in the old Cemetery of San Juan, near the tomb of the poet and patriot José de Diego, at the foot of El Morro's centenary walls. After his death, as happens in those cases, the figure of Albizu Campos has achieved even greater stature, as a symbol of the real Puerto Rico. Today, at the end of 1965, his phrase that "one's country is courage and sacrifice" is being widely adopted as a motto by a considerable number of young Puerto Ricans.

As this book goes to press, we know that two serious and well-documented studies of the dead patriot are being written: one by Dr. Manuel Maldonado Denis, professor of Political Science at the University of Puerto Rico, and the other by the poet Juan Antonio Corretjer. We still lack, nevertheless, a complete collection, with authoritative notes and historical annotations, of the speeches, public declarations, letters, and newspaper interviews of the political leader and jurist Pedro Albizu Campos, in order to give Puerto Rico and the world the true meaning and importance of his thought. We think that the most suitable person for such an enormous scholarly task is the Puerto Rican historian Dr. Isabel Gutiérrez del Arroyo, and that, as a matter of historical justice, Dr. Gutiérrez del Arroyo's future work should be sponsored and financed by the Instituto de Cultura Puertorriqueña or—why not?— by the College of Lawyers of Puerto Rico. We are, after all, dealing with one of its most distinguished and certainly with one of its most internationally famous and admired colleagues. (After this note was written, at the end of 1965, we read in 1966 Dr. Manuel Maldonado Denis' work on Albizu and we must confess that it disappointed us. We hopefully await that of the poet, Juan Antonio Corretjer, Albizu's companion. Apart from these, we insist upon the importance of the work which could be done by Dr. Isabel Gutiérrez del Arroyo.)

21. At the end of the last century the North American Constitution and its Bill of Rights (the latter incorporated as an imitation of the fundamental document of the French Revolution) were the sun which dazzled many Puerto Rican liberals: a natural reaction to the long years of authoritarian rule under Spanish domination. Their dazzlement by the democratic principles of the North American nation prevented some Puerto Ricans from clearly examining sociopolitical realities and obvious imperialist tendencies which admirers of and believers in democracy such as Martí and Betances did not fail to perceive in the powerful organism of the United States of North America. It was in this way that a handful of autonomists and separatists under the Spanish regime, who did not have the vision of Martí, became, with the change in Puerto Rican sovereignty, the first proponents of annexationism or statehood-ism under the North American regime. Moreover, at the beginning of the century, the men who defended statehood believed in good faith that they were dealing with a purely political problem. The possibility of the moral, cultural, and

spiritual destruction of a people by psychological means was an idea foreign to some cultured Puerto Ricans of that time. Now that the century has progressed, however, and has put two world wars behind it, the moral coercion of propaganda has been elevated to the status of a science, and the techniques of psychological aggression have been raised to their most subtle level of refinement. The brain washing and spiritual manipulation of individuals and nations are tangible realities from which man cannot escape in the atomic age. In this era of "supercivilization," unknown to the annexationists at the beginning of the century, moral, cultural, and spiritual destruction at the hands of a dominating nation is a more *real and immediate* menace for a nation than the obsolete destruction by physical means.

22. It seems unnecessary to point out that as soon as the North American Department of State opened fire on the Cuban Revolutionary Government, the Fidelist enthusiasm of these Puerto Rican intellectuals rapidly faded away. Today Pan American bureaucratic planners in Washington can count on no more steadfast opponents of Fidel than they.

23. On a non-literary level the historian Isabel Gutiérrez del Arroyo has made a very neat attempt to clarify annexationism in her *Razones de una Sinrazón*, a work originally published in the newspaper *El Mundo* (1959) and then printed in the form of pamphlet under the title of *¿Puerto Rico Estado Federado?* (Barcelona: Imprenta Suño, 1960).

24. Supporter or present sponsor would be more exact. Already in 1922 the Union Party of Puerto Rico, oriented ideologically until his death, a few years before, by Luis Muñoz Rivera, had included this political compromise in its platform, and under the same name. Twenty years later, in 1942, three Puerto Ricans who were active in the Popular Democratic Party then in power (Rafael Cordero, Enrique Campos del Toro, and Miguel Guerra Mondragón) proposed to the then North American governor of the island, Rexford G. Tugwell, the old reformist formula of the Union Party. They alleged that the Puerto Rican people were not yet ready for statehood and that the Commonwealth would serve as a preparation for future statehood. (This revelation was made by one of the guiding thinkers of annexationism today, the ex-liberal and ex-progressive Rexford G. Tugwell, in his book, *The Art of Politics* [New York: Doubleday, 1958.]) In one way or another it was not until 1952 that the compromise measure, conceived by the three Puerto Ricans mentioned above as a transitional stage toward statehood, became reality under the leadership of Luis Muñoz Marín. Muñoz Rivera's political legacy, taken up by his son, was thirty years in consolidating itself as the psychological expression of the Puerto Rican people today.

25. *Translator's note:* This is the noun form of *ñangotado*. See note 9, above.

26. José A. Balseiro, *En Vela Mientras el Mundo Duerme* (San Juan: Biblioteca de Autores Puertorriqueños, 1953.)

27. After publication of that work in 1956, however, this author seems to have evolved ideologically toward a position favoring independence.

28. A similar psychological mechanism—the identification with official authoritarianism—operates in almost the entire colony of North Americans in Puerto Rico. It can be seen most clearly in the recent arrivals—technicians, experts, professionals, foremen, salesmen, hotel men, industrialists, real estate speculators, bankers, administrators, and businessmen—all of those, finally, who constitute the second and in all ways more devastating invasion.

29. It is not that this is an exclusively Puerto Rican phenomenon, but since it is Puerto Rico that concerns us, the demanding specialists will excuse us if we spare them, and ourselves, any digressions on the same situation in other contemporary societies which, if we may be pardoned, matter much less to us than our own. To express it in the pic-

turesque argot of the Industrial Development Company: "Let every mast support its own sail."

30. *La Llamarada* (1st ed.; Aguadilla, P.R.: Tipografía Ruiz, 1935). *Tiempo Muerto* (1st ed.; San Juan: Publicaciones Areyto, 1940). *Usmaíl* (San Juan: Club del Libro de Puerto Rico, 1959). *La Muerte No Entrará en Palacio*. In *Teatro* (Mexico: Ediciones Arrecife, 1959).

31. See the prologue to *Cuentos Puertorriqueños de Hoy* (San Juan: Club del Libro de Puerto Rico, 1959).

32. See the short story "En la popa hay un cuerpo reclinado" in the anthology mentioned above.

33. We make a point of the adjective *social* because we have absolutely no intention of introducing the reader to the confused field of pedagogy.

34. This fact—the swearing of allegiance to the North American flag by Puerto Ricans—has been reflected in our literature. It was dramatized in the already mentioned short story "El Juramento" by René Marqués (1955) and more recently (1959) in a novel by the same author, *La Víspera del Hombre* (ch. 18).

35. A superficial glance at the civic organizations in Puerto Rico seems to indicate that, in terms of their Americanization, the Lions are less Americanized than the Rotarians, while the Elks achieve the highest level of Americanization possible. (A curious fact: the Elks are embarassed to translate their name into Spanish. This bashfulness is inexplicable since in our language elks are simply "alces," "antas," or, as they are defined in any Spanish dictionary, "ruminant quadrupeds similar to the deer and as corpulent as the horse." We can see that being identified as "ruminant quadrupeds" is not something which would flatter the collective ego of a fraternal organization, but terms of fauna such as "alces" or "antas" are as decorous in Spanish as that of lions, and are all capable of symbolizing the noble spirit of civism and human fraternity of these North American organizations in Puerto Rico today.) The civic ladies, for their part, seem to occupy, in the Americanist scale, an intermediate place between the Lions and the Rotarians. (A curious fact: the civic ladies do not swear allegiance to the American flag in their regular ceremonies. Why in this case the civic women do not do the same as the civic men will always be difficult to determine. One might, however, ask: Are the women *less* docile than the men? Within a matriarchal society it would seem logical to suppose so.)

Translator's note: The greeting is in English in the original text.

36. Paradoxically, Protestantism, a recent import from North American culture, though it has contributed to the deterioration and disentegration of Puerto Rican national unity, has not had much to do, at least in its direct religious activity, with the social imposition of English. This is perhaps due to the fact that the immense majority of the Portestant heirarchy, clergy, and leadership is Puerto Rican. One must not forget, however, that in the last fifty years it has been Protestants, occupying key positions in the Department of Education and in the island legislature, who have attacked the vernacular most determinedly and have defended most fervidly linguistic North Americanization through public education in Puerto Rico.

In the general way, much the same thing can be said about Masonry, whose leaders are Puerto Rican, but whose lodges are almost all branches of the central power in the United States, from which they receive a North American nationalist orientation in open conflict with the possible survival of the Puerto Rican nationality. Even the Spiritists, whose kingdom would seem to be less of this world than that of other religious groups, cannot avoid feeling, in the Great Beyond, somewhat bewildered about Puerto Rico's political-cultural problem. Thus, Puerto Rican believers in Spiritism today have to hear their grandparents and great grandparents speak to them from beyond the grave in North American English with a Brooklyn or Middle West accent, even though they had died in the times of the Spanish rule. Perhaps this is due to the fact that often the best and most famous mediums who operate in the Puerto Rican sessions are North Americans. (The author was assured by a famous North American medium in San Juan that his maestro— a spiritual godfather or protector, we suppose—was the English writer Carlyle. The gratuitous godson was not as surprised by the fact that in a few seconds his unchosen maestro began to speak with a New York accent, as by the fact that, in spite of there being so many Spanish-speaking writers wandering in the stellar spaces, they should have to assign him in the other world one so annoying and typically British as Carlyle. This only goes to show the tremendous cultural confusion which we Puerto Ricans are condemned to suffer even beyond the frontiers of our already confused material life.

37. *Translator's note:* The Spanish word for a retreat is *retiro.*

38. We refer to the University of Puerto Rico (a public institution subsidized and oriented by the state). In the two private universities—the Catholic one of Santa María in Ponce and the Protestant Interamerican University in San Germán—the imposition of English is carried to ridiculous extremes. Moreover, in a good number of the Catholic schools in the island, the teaching is done completely in English, thus violating the regulations of the Department of Public Education. This does not seem to bother at all the officials of this government agency charged with authorizing and regulating the operating of private schools in Puerto Rico.

39. Since docility must be considered more an acquired characteristic than a hereditary or congenital evil, a strongly anticolonialist system of public education could in two or three generation markedly change the psycho-social picture of Puerto Rican docility. Unfortunately, it is this type of education which the Puerto Rican people will never be permitted to have in their present colonial situation. The proof of this assertion can be seen in what has become of the pretentious "educational reform"—a confession of the most complete pedagogical impotence within the present colonial system.

40. See Amaury de Reincourt, *The Coming Caesar* (New York: Coward-McCann, 1957).

41. This is an allusion to some verses of Lola Rodríguez de Tió, a Puerto Rican poet of the past century: "Cuba and Puerto Rico are / of one bird, the two wings; / they receive flowers and bullets / in the same heart." Toward the middle of 1966 Fidel Castro, in one of his fiery speeches, made a tremendous blunder and attributed these verses to José Martí. Is Fidel proposing to go so far as to nationalize *our* poetry?

42. The complex also operates, although to a lesser degree, when he confronts other Westerners, especially Spaniards (precisely those who occupied at one time the place which the North American occupies today). Spaniards continue fostering in Puerto Rican artistic and cultural life certain bad habits dear to the island colonial complexes. Look at the number of Spanish mediocrities who occupy key positions among the artistic and cultural elite and in university circles. Even before the figures of those few Spanish residents of real and undeniable intellectual worth, the general attitude of the Puerto Rican is not one of dignified acknowledgement, but rather of a certain tropical servility, as if his ancestral servitude under the Conquistador had reappeared. The insulting farcical scenes put on by certain Puerto Rican circles for prestigious figures like Juan Ramón Jiménez and Pablo Casals perhaps give an idea of what we mean. On the other hand, in the so-called social life, the Casa de España (the Spanish Club) continues to fascinate, as a supreme goal, a great number of middle-class San Juan residents. In the younger generations, better indoctrinated in North American national prejudices, the colonial complex is

disguised by an air of superiority shown toward citizens of so-called "underdeveloped" countries. This arbitrary designation includes Antilleans (Puerto Ricans are apparently exempted from that category), Latin Americans, Africans, and Asiatics. The new Puerto Rican struts before these human beings classified as "inferior" by the North Americans, making an ostentatious display of his mended colonial plumage. It is an innocent and superficial attitude most of the time, but it can be truly vicious in cases of extreme North Americanization.

43. It can be noted as a curious fact that Puerto Rican escapism also functions in the discipline of philosophy. University students, disoriented perhaps by the prejudices which they hear mediocre teachers express in some philosophy courses, wander through the campus denying that they are Puerto Ricans. "What is this of *being* Puerto Ricans?"— they indignantly protest—"*Being* is a philosophic concept which goes from Thales of Miletus to Hegel and which has absolutely nothing to do with any nationality. No one, but no one can *be* Puerto Rican!" When one is faced with the ineffable I.Q.'s of these child philosophers, it is not even worth the trouble to send them to the classic statement of Ortega: "I am myself plus my circumstance, and if I do not save it, I cannot save myself." It is obvious that for them, poor souls who unaware of Being pass through life without even *being,* there is no possible salvation.

44. *Translator's note:* The Spanish saying is "Courtesy does not imply a lack of valor."

45. The escapist tendency of the beatniks has respectable precedents in North American literature. Remember that in the contemporary world the United States is perhaps the only country which produces again and again the phenomenon of the writer who voluntarily expatriates himself, even at times renouncing his North American citizenship. In the last century Henry James was the first notable example of this. He was followed at the beginning of this century by T. S. Eliot, today a British subject resident in England. The phenomenon culminates dramatically in the Lost Generation of the first postwar period, a group headed by Ernest Hemingway, which decided to settle in the French capitol. Hemingway never completely renounced his condition of self-exile. After long sojourns in Europe, Spain, and Africa, he established his residence in Cuba, apparently identifying himself with the fate of the Cuban people until a serious illness forced him to return to his country of origin for medical treatment. Significantly, his stay there was not long. During a period of mental illness, a rifle shot, obviously self-inflicted, put an end to his incurable disenchantment with the society in which he had been born.

46. This aspect of the writer's mission has been explored in the essay, "Literary Pessimism and Political Optimism: Their Coexistence in Contemporary Puerto Rico," included in this volume.

47. We have used this phrase without defining it, but perhaps it is necessary to do so now. We think, along with various contemporary psychologists, that each society has a guilt complex caused by what we could call its "original sin." In the case of Puerto Rico it seems obvious that its colonial situation is the sin which gives birth to the guilt complex. Although we can identify it as a subconscious motive, it does not appear in our literature in an articulated or reasoned form. We would have to go to Jean Paul Sartre's tragedy *The Flies,* to observe a collective guilt complex embodied in dramatic form. In fact, in the Sartrean existentialist tragedy, the plague of flies which destroys the city-state of Argos symbolizes the guilt feelings of the town which has on its conscience the ancestral crimes of the Atridas family.

48. In recent years, and even before the disappearance of the minority Independence Party, when the crisis of the independence movement atomized its sparse forces in an in-

finite number of antagonistic groups, the reaction of the Popular ex-"independentistas" to this historic occurrence is an excellent lesson of applied psychology. Instead of celebrating with delight the decadence of the ideology which they betrayed and to whose destruction they contributed so much from their present position as Commonwealth partisans, they were in some cases sincerely desolate, and in others merely sorrowful, and a good number of them turned furiously against the "independentistas," not for being independentistas, but for being bad independentistas. In other words, they criticized them for not having known how to achieve an electoral triumph for the independence movement. The situation brings immediately to mind Díaz Valcárcel's story mentioned above about the Puerto Rican in Korea. These ex-independentista Popular Democrats, just like the soldier Damián Sánchez, instead of giving vent to their humiliation and frustration as Puerto Ricans in the only rational and logical way in which it could be done, relieved their wrath viciously and uselessly on those whom they considered to be more humiliated and frustrated as human beings than they themselves.

49. This alludes to a line of Luis Palés Matos: "Puerto Rico: Burundanga."

Translator's note: The word *burundanga* means a conglomeration of unrelated and ill-matched things. Used ironically it implies—nothing.

50. El Español en Puerto Rico (San Juan: Editorial Universidad de Puerto Rico, 1948).

51. The two appendices were written later (1965-66), for the inclusion of "The Docile Puerto Rican" in the essay collection.

52. At this very moment the Puerto Rican Pro-Independence Movement has publicly accused the C.I.A. of being the intellectual author of the fire (obviously a case of arson) which recently destroyed the central offices of the group's National Mission in Río Piedras. Also destroyed were three oil paintings on patriotic themes—two by Fran Cervoni and the third by Antonio Maldonado—valued at about twenty thousand dollars. The investigation by the authorities is continuing, but we doubt very much that, if the Pro Independence Movement's public allegation were proven true—something very difficult to prove, of course, considering the C.I.A. involvement—the local government would have the courage to place official responsibility for the terrorist act upon the all powerful C.I.A. in Puerto Rico. There would be, in that case, an adequate "sacrificial lamb" to satisfy appearances, and to protect both the sinister secrecy of the C.I.A. in our country and the "prestige" of the colonial Puerto Rican government.

53. Although the F.B.I. also devotes itself to criminal investigation, its principal function in Puerto Rico is that of political repression.

54. This agency has principally one mission: that of investigating draftees, especially if they are "independentistas" and more especially if they belong to the so-called radical groups, or if the young citizen shows reluctance or open opposition to fighting in wars which *his* country has not declared. Since Puerto Ricans must go to fight North American wars in foreign countries without being represented in the Federal Congress (we have there a Resident Commissioner of Puerto Rico with a voice—when Congress courteously concedes it—but without *any vote;* a mere lobbyist in other words), we could parody the Fathers of the Great Republic of North America and affirm that "a tribute of blood—the most valuable one that a human being can give—without representation, is tyranny" (or pure colonialism, which is the same thing). It goes without saying that various non-docile Puerto Ricans have been jailed for having refused to serve in the North American army.

55. In close collaboration with another non-Puerto Rican repressive force, the Department of State of Washington, and basing themselves on a very extensive, encyclopedic, and exhaustive "black list," Federal Immigration dictates, both to Puerto Ricans

themselves and to foreigners who visit or wish to visit our country, *who* can enter or leave Puerto Rico as well as *how* and *when*. (In the case of Puerto Ricans, they are also told precisely *where* they can or cannot go, if Washington gives them a passport to leave the island.) The local government has no power to counteract or even to alleviate this humiliating situation. There have been cases of distinguished foreigners or Puerto Ricans—the eminent Puerto Rican actor José Ferrer, among them—who have been official guests of the Government of Puerto Rico and still suffered unspeakable annoyances at the hands of Federal Immigration or Customs agents.

56. No one can deny that the North American postal service operating on the island is one of the most efficient and rapid in the world. This does not mean that it is exempt— like so many ones in various modern countries—from involuntary or voluntary faults, including censorship. This latter, in private first-class correspondence, only operates *officially* in times of war. But the Postal Service, in collaboration with the Federal Customs, daily uses censorship to make difficult or, if possible, to prevent the introduction and circulation in the colony of foreign magazines and books, and even of literature *by Puerto Rican authors* published outside the island. There is more, however. In the internal mail system—between the cities and towns of the island—there have been not infrequent cases of postmasters and postmistresses who have mysteriously retained dozens of small magazines or newspapers of "independentista" groups, properly stamped and with clear and correct addresses, which had been sent to their affiliates or members. The criteria for such a "democratic" task, both in the Postal Service and in the Customs, are primarily *political,* but one or the other of them on occasion permit themselves the luxury of basing their repression on a "moral" issue. The most ridiculous and stupid action in this respect has to do with a book of Puerto Rican folklore published in Spain by the Institute of Puerto Rican Culture, an agency of the Puerto Rican government, and whose author is . . . a North American! (*Folklore Puertorriqueño: Adivinanzas,* by J. Alden Mason.) The Federal Customs withheld the book because it considered it "pornographic." The distrubance caused by such scandalous stupidity forced the censors of the Federal Customs to rectify their attitude, and they finally permitted the entrance and circulation of the book in Puerto Rico. On occasion foreign books or magazines which can be gotten without difficulty in any bookstore or newspaper stand in New York or San Francisco (and which some Puerto Ricans even receive fairly regularly by mail) do not seem to be able to circulate *freely,* through public sale, in bookstores and newstands in Puerto Rico. It is difficult for us to determine as we write these lines whether this is due to Customs or Postal censorship or to a cowardly and self-imposed censorship of docile Puerto Rican booksellers and magazine and newspapers distributors. (Someone—the inactive Committee on Civil Liberties, the College of Lawyers, John Doe?—with more time than we have at this moment, should begin an adequate investigation of this esoteric problem.)

57. The Federal Communications Commission dominates from Washington not only the concession of licenses to operate local radio and television stations, but also, through its regulations, can—and it has done so in specific instances—restrict free political expression in these mass communications media in Puerto Rico. (It should also be made clear that the Federal Communications Commission has not permitted, up to now, the establishment in our country of a short wave station, that is, one of sufficient strength to make itself heard beyond the narrow limits of the island and the Antilles.) Also, some local owners of radio and television stations, fearful, justifiably or not, of losing their license from Washington, are quite careful—sometimes too much so—about selling time to minority "independentista" groups, especially to the so-called radical or "subversive" ones. Is this complete freedom of expression in the "showcase of democracy"? The reader

must judge. Or, to be rigorously exact, Washington, D.C. will be the judge. *Roma locuta, causa finita.*

58. Internal Security imitates the methods of the F.B.I., although with greater stupidity and less effectiveness than the federal agency.

59. The most recent and obvious pressure from the aggressive and upstart minority of Cuban exiles in our country to which the local government has yielded is related to the celebration of the Central American and Caribbean Games in 1966. After Puerto Rico had been selected for the first time as the seat for this important sports event, and after Washington had given assurances that it would give visas to the Cuban participants, the local government alleged that the Cubans could not participate since it would be very difficult, if not impossible, for the Puerto Rican authorities to guarantee the lives of "Castro's" players during their stay in the country. One should note not only the terrible ignorance about the rules of international sports, but the strange, incredible, inconceivable, ridiculous excuse of a local government which can count on the greatest number of repressive forces (both federal and local) in this hemisphere to guarantee "peace" and "order" within the small geographic size of its country. The ridiculous scandal has caused such repercussions that, because of the valiant protest of the Puerto Rican athletes (who are certainly not, in the majority, Castroists) and because of pressure from Washington (upon whom part of the ridicule and discredit for such an unusual action would fall), it now seems very probable that Puerto Rico will be the seat of the athletic event with the participation, naturally, of the Cuban athletes.

60. *Translator's note:* A *cuerda* is a Puerto Rican agricultural measurement equivalent to 4,000 square meters.

61. Some Puerto Ricans believe, or pretend to believe, that the whole military complex on the island, built up after the invasion of 1898, is very "generously" maintained here by the United States to "protect" *our country* from hypothetical invaders. Martians, perhaps? Puerto Rican ingenuousness can reach, on occasions, a pathetic level.

62. *Translator's note: Comecandelismo* is a tendency to act or speak boldly for the sake of being bold rather than for the results accomplished.

The Puerto Rican Short Story of the Forties Generation

1. The author has enlarged upon the study of this problem in his essay "Literary Pessimism and Political Optimism: Their Coexistence in Contemporary Puerto Rico," included in this volume.

2. United Nations, *Demographic Yearbook, 1951.* Apart from what is indicated above about Catholic countries, Puerto Rico occupies fourth place in the list of the five countries with the highest annual suicide rates in the world.

3. Remember that this was written at the end of 1959.

4. Living in a colony, they probably identify the word with "political chicanery."

5. Of the group mentioned when the essay was written in 1959, only Luis Rafael Sánchez has excelled as a good short story writer, besides his accomplishments as a playwright. Because of his age, this writer could, however, be considered rather as a transitional figure between the forties and the fifties generations. The latter has so far shown exceptional talent only in poetry. However, the outline of a younger generation, although blurred, is beginning to appear, one almost adolescent now and mostly unpublished—the future generation of the sixties perhaps. Some of its members show adequate talent and dedication in the prose genres, particularly the short story. We optimistically await its "official" appearance on the literary horizon. Time will judge its fruits.

6. In the local monthly magazine written in English. The *San Juan Review,* there were published, in 1964 and 1965, English translations of short stories by José Luis González, Pedro Juan Soto, René Marqués, Edwin Figueroa, Emilio Díaz Valcárcel, Abelardo Díaz Alfaro, and Salvador de Jesús. Nina Kaiden, Pedro Juan Soto, and Andrew Vladimir, eds., *Puerto Rico: La Nueva Vida; The New Life* (Bilingual ed.; New York: Renaissance Editions, 1966), has short fragments of writings of Salvador de Jesús, José Luis González, Edwin Figueroa, René Marqués, Pedro Juan Soto and Emilio Díaz Valcárcel.

A Character in Folklore and a Theme of Farce in Puerto Rico

1. *Translator's note:* The word *bobo* means fool, simpleton.

2. *Translator's note: Bumelia nigra,* native to the Antilles.

Message of a Puerto Rican to the Writers and Artists of Peru

1. A Colombian newspaper closed by the government at about that time.

2. Then president of Costa Rica.

The Function of the Puerto Rican Writer Today

1. A member of the audience, a young Puerto Rican priest, acutely observed that when the writer rejects all absolute truths, he is at that moment proclaiming an absolute truth. That is so. One must clarify, however, that the writer only claims to question absolute truths in relation to the act of creation. He can, as a citizen, have embraced with sincere faith an absolute truth. An example of this is the Catholic writer Graham Greene, who, in his novels, questions, or appears to many Catholics to be questioning, some aspects of the absolute truth in which, as an individual, he honorably believes. The profound truth which the writer brings to light in his creative work is the result of the contradictions which he observes in the world around him and even, at times, in the religious or political doctrines with which he has identified himself.

2. A Catholic group in the audience objected to this affirmation, alleging that there are cases in which the writer adapts himself or conforms, unrebelliously, to a specific ideology or doctrine. As an example of this the case of Claudel was brought up. I accept the validity of the objection—the exceptions confirm the rule—but I consider the example of Claudel a weak one. In a liberal France, where even Catholicism has achieved a degree of liberalism which shocks Rome, Claudel's act of regression in embracing and expressing in his works an almost medieval Catholicism can be interpreted to a great degree as a protest against his environment, as an act of rebellion, in fact, whether we are in agreement with him or not. The degree of rebellion of the writer and the way in which he expresses it will depend, naturally, as much on the historic circumstances of the society in which he lives, as on his own temperament and personal circumstances.

3. The danger for the creative artist in the indefinite prolongation of the subtle distinction between the revolution and the state, made by the leaders of revolutionary states, was seen very tangibly in the Soviet Union. It is clearly reasonable for a revolution to ask the writer and the artist to suspend temporarily their freedom of creation during the initial revolutionary period. But the Soviet state made the temporary suspension a permanent one, prolonging it for almost forty years—the whole lifetime of a writer or an artist—and always in the name of the revolution. Only now in the post-Stalinist period has the Soviet state began to concede some freedom of expression to the writer, both in form and in content. This is why Soviet literature has been of such poor quality during those four decades, annulling or only precariously fulfilling both its esthetic and its social functions.

Index